MW00352357

LOST CHURCHES

of

MISSISSIPPI

The second building of Crawford Street Methodist Episcopal Church in Vicksburg, as it appeared about 1900.

LOST CHURCHES

of

MISSISSIPPI

RICHARD J. CAWTHON

University Press of Mississippi
Jackson

This book is dedicated to my parents
James D. Cawthon and Juanita Davis Cawthon.

www.upress.state.ms.us

Designed by Peter D. Halverson

The University Press of Mississippi is a member
of the Association of American University Presses.

Copyright © 2010 by University Press of Mississippi
All rights reserved
Printed in Canada

First printing 2010

∞

Library of Congress Cataloging-in-Publication Data

Cawthon, Richard J.
Lost churches of Mississippi / Richard J. Cawthon.
p. cm.
Includes bibliographical references and index.
ISBN 978-1-60473-436-2 (cloth : alk. paper) 1. Church buildings—Mississipppi.
2. Lost architecture—Mississippi. I. Cawthon, Richard J.
NA5230.M6 C39 2010
726.509762—dc22   2009040406

British Library Cataloging-in-Publication Data available

Contents

Preface and Acknowledgments

This book is a collection of photographs, postcards, and other images of architecturally interesting old churches and synagogues of Mississippi that no longer stand. One hundred and ten lost churches and synagogues are featured here. This is only a small portion of buildings that could have been included. Those selected were churches or synagogues for which good, reproducible images were available—mostly from the photographic collections of the Mississippi Department of Archives and History (MDAH)—and for which some historical information could be readily obtained, mostly from the files of the Historic Preservation Division, MDAH. Numerous other buildings equally worthy of attention were left out only because photographs or other images suitable for making high-resolution digital scans were not available or because not enough historical information could be assembled in time to use it in the book. I regret that I was unable to spend much time examining materials in the reference collections of local libraries, museums, and historical societies around the state. From the libraries and archival collections that I did have the opportunity to consult during the preparation of this book, I was able to obtain sufficient information to document this limited number of particularly interesting lost buildings—but these few buildings are only a small sampling of the many churches and synagogues of Mississippi that no longer stand.

The Historic Preservation Division of MDAH maintains an extensive and ever-growing set of files about the historic buildings of the state, including non-extant buildings. If readers of this book have additional information about lost churches in their communities, I urge them to bring that information to the attention of the architectural historians on the staff of the Historic Preservation Division.

This book is intended primarily as a pictorial work. The emphasis is on the illustrations. I have endeavored to provide architectural information about each building to enable the reader to appreciate the buildings within their historical and architectural contexts, but I have not intended to provide a narrative history of the buildings or their congregations. This book is a celebration of their architecture, expressed largely through old photographs.

Documenting the architecture of buildings that no longer survive is much more challenging than documenting existing buildings. One cannot visit a lost building to photograph it, examine it, and describe its appearance. Instead, the researcher must depend upon old drawings and photographs and other sources of pictorial information, such as Sanborn fire insurance maps and bird's-eye town maps. Old postcards are particularly helpful sources. At the back of this book are three compilations of reference sources that are intended to assist readers who are interested in doing further reading and research on the lost churches of Mississippi. The first is a collection of endnotes listing sources used for the text and offering further explanations and comments. The second reference compilation is an annotated bibliography that includes an introductory commentary on sources of information about the history of religious architecture in Mississippi. The third is a detailed list of the sources of the illustrations used in the book.

The inspiration for compiling this book came from several sources. It was partly inspired by my experience of working for twenty years as the chief architectural historian for the Mississippi Department of Archives and History, a position I held from August of 1985 until my retirement at the end of January 2006. During that time, in the course of reorganizing and adding extensive documentation to a system of files about thousands of buildings and historic sites throughout the state, I realized that those files contained information about hundreds of architecturally notable buildings that no longer stand. A more immediate inspiration was the publication of Mary Carol Miller's *Lost Mansions of Mississippi* and *Lost Landmarks of Mississippi*, which brought many of the state's lost buildings to the attention of the reading public. The strongest inspiration for this book, however, was the experience of working with photographer Sherry Pace to produce the book *Historic Churches of Mississippi*, which was published by the University Press of Mississippi in 2007. As I did the research and wrote the text for that book, I came to realize that the existing churches and synagogues of Mississippi embody only part of the history of the state's religious architecture. In order to truly appreciate the architectural context of the historic religious buildings that still stand, one must also have some knowledge about religious buildings that no longer exist.

This book would not have been possible without the assistance and encouragement of many people and institutions. I am indebted, first and foremost, to my parents, Mr. and Mrs. James D. Cawthon, for their boundless support and encouragement. Special thanks are due to Craig Gill, assistant director and editor-in-chief of the University Press of Mississippi, who urged me to write the book and provided immeasurable guidance and direction. I would also like to thank my former colleagues in the Historic Preservation Division of the Mississippi Department of Archives and History, especially Jennifer Baughn and Todd Sanders; the staff of the Archives and Records Services Division of MDAH, particularly Anne Webster, Clinton Bagley, Joyce Dixon-Lawson, Grady Howell, De'Nieceschi Layton, Jeff Rogers, and Michael Allard; Jeffrey H. Coleman of the Old Court House Museum in Vicksburg; Dr. Stuart Rockoff of the Goldring/ Woldenberg Institute of Southern Jewish Life, Jackson; Mary Woodward of the Catholic Diocese of Jackson; Laurie Crowson of the Hattiesburg Area Historical Society; Mimi Miller of the Historic Natchez Foundation; Mrs. Joseph Sanders of Corinth (mother of my friend and colleague Todd Sanders); Dan Stockton of Jackson; and Pamela Williamson of the J. D. Williams Library at the University of Mississippi. In addition, I appreciate the assistance of Cherie Ester of Ithaca Baptist Church, Ithaca, Michigan; Diane Mallstrom of the Public Library of Cincinnati and Hamilton County, Cincinnati, Ohio; James T. Wollon, Jr., AIA, of Havre de Grace, Maryland; and Stephen Yates of the State Archives of Florida, Tallahassee, Florida. Lastly I wish to offer a special thanks to Mary Carol Miller for the inspiration and encouragement to compile this book.

Introduction

Churches and synagogues are often among the most visually prominent and architecturally interesting buildings in any American community. That is certainly true of the cities and towns of Mississippi. They are often among the most historically interesting buildings as well, but many of the most architecturally and historically interesting religious buildings no longer exist, having been destroyed or remodeled beyond recognition. This book is intended to showcase a selection of some of the more notable of the lost churches and synagogues of Mississippi.

Lost Churches of Mississippi is primarily a collection of photographs and other illustrations depicting those lost churches, along with some architectural and historical information about them. There is also some information about the broader architectural context of a few of the churches, but this book is not intended to be a *history* of religious architecture in Mississippi. Readers seeking an overview of the architectural history of Mississippi churches are urged to consult the historical summary "Religious Architecture in Mississippi from the 1820s through the 1920s," which serves as the introduction to *Historic Churches of Mississippi.*

All of the churches and synagogues featured in this book are "lost" in the sense that the buildings have been destroyed or remodeled beyond recognition. Only one of these churches still stands (the old First Baptist Church of Corinth), and it is now in a largely unrecognizable form, having been converted to a commercial building. All the others are completely gone, having been lost due to a variety of different causes.

Many of Mississippi's lost churches were destroyed by storms. Some were lost to tornadoes, such as the old St. Paul's Catholic Church in Vicksburg, which was severely damaged by the tornado that ripped though the downtown in December

1953, and Bethel Presbyterian Church near Columbus, which was destroyed by a tornado in 2002. Many churches along the Gulf Coast have been damaged or destroyed by hurricanes, most notably Hurricane Camille in 1969 and Hurricane Katrina in 2005. Hurricane Camille caused the destruction of the old Trinity Episcopal Church and the old St. Paul's Catholic Church in Pass Christian, the old St. John's Catholic Church in Gulfport, and the second building of the Church of the Redeemer in Biloxi. Thirty-six years later, Hurricane Katrina destroyed St. Mark's Episcopal Church in Gulfport and the older building of the Church of the Redeemer, among numerous other churches.

Some churches have been lost to fires, including the old First Presbyterian Church in Yazoo City, which was destroyed in the fire that ravaged the downtown in 1904, and the second building of Crawford Street Methodist Church in Vicksburg, which burned in 1925.

A surprisingly large proportion of Mississippi's lost religious buildings were demolished at the behest of their own congregations, either because they were perceived to be structurally unsound or because the congregation desired to construct a larger building or one in a different location. The old First Baptist Church of Biloxi, the old First Presbyterian Church of Corinth, the old St. James Episcopal Church in Greenville, the old First Baptist Church of Hattiesburg, both the second and third buildings of Temple Beth Israel in Jackson, the old Central Methodist Church in Meridian, and the old First Baptist Church in Yazoo City were among the many churches and synagogues that were sold or demolished when their congregations erected buildings at new locations. The Methodist Church in Brandon, the old First Baptist Church of Columbus, and the old First Methodist Church of Greenville were among those that were demolished in order to be replaced by a new house of worship at the same site as the earlier building. In some cases a new sanctuary was constructed immediately next door to the old one, which sometimes continued to serve as an annex, chapel, or fellowship hall for some time until it was demolished, as was the case with the First Baptist Church in Amory. (A surviving example of this practice of retaining an older sanctuary as an annex or fellowship hall can be seen at First Presbyterian Church in Greenwood, where a new sanctuary was built in 1925–26 immediately next to the old sanctuary, dating from 1904, which was remodeled to serve as a church annex.)

Some religious buildings, such as the Clear Creek Baptist Church near Natchez, were simply abandoned when their congregation moved or became defunct, and the buildings eventually fell into ruin.

For many lost churches, however, the cause of their loss has not been documented in readily available published sources, though in some cases documentation about the cause of destruction can be found locally, in the records of the congregation or in a local archival collection. Sometimes records of the destruction of a church building can be found in the minutes of a local church governing board, in the reports of the annual conventions of regional church associations, or in local newspapers. (The author would be very grateful to any readers who could provide information about the circumstances surrounding the loss of any of the churches in this book.)

Regardless of the cause of their destruction, the lost churches of Mississippi are an important but largely unrecognized part of the architectural heritage of the state. This book is intended to enable some of those lost churches and synagogues to receive some recognition and appreciation. It is hoped that the book will inspire readers to discover more of the lost architectural and historic landmarks of their communities.

LOST CHURCHES

of

MISSISSIPPI

ABERDEEN

First Methodist Church (1859–60)
First Baptist Church (circa 1891–94)

AMORY

First Methodist Church (1914)
First Baptist Church (1918)

BAY ST. LOUIS

Church of Our Lady of the Gulf (1872)

BELZONI

First Baptist Church (1922)

BILOXI

(First) Church of the Redeemer (1873–74)
(Second) Church of the Redeemer (1891)
Main Street Methodist Church (1904–5)
First Baptist Church (1924)

BOONEVILLE

First Methodist Church (1897)

BRANDON

Brandon Methodist Church (1867–73)

BROOKHAVEN
First Methodist Church (1904)

BUENA VISTA
Presbyterian Church (later Baptist Church) (1860)

CANTON
Presbyterian Church (1852–53)
Temple B'nai Israel (1877)

CLARKSDALE
First Methodist Church (1897)
First Presbyterian Church (circa 1915–17)
First Christian Church (1923–29)

COLLINS
Baptist Church (1925)

COLUMBIA
First Baptist Church (1911–12)

COLUMBUS AND VICINITY
First Baptist Church (1838–40)
Bethel Presbyterian Church (1844–45)

CORINTH
First Methodist Church (1890–92)
First Baptist Church (1894–95)
First Presbyterian Church (1894–96)

CRYSTAL SPRINGS
Crystal Springs Methodist Church (1919)

DREW
Drew Baptist Church (1920)

DURANT
First Baptist Church (1898)

EDWARDS
Edwards Methodist Church (1899)

GREENVILLE
St. James Episcopal Church (1885–86)
First Presbyterian Church (1901–2)
First Methodist Church (1903–4)
First Baptist Church (1906–7)

GREENWOOD
First Baptist Church (1907–10)

GRENADA
First Baptist Church (1888–91)

GULFPORT
St. Mark's Episcopal Church (1855)
First Baptist Church (1915)
St. John the Evangelist Catholic Church (1922–24)

HATTIESBURG
Main Street Presbyterian Church (1887, 1900)
Sacred Heart Catholic Church (1900)
First Baptist Church (circa 1901)

HAZLEHURST
Hazlehurst Baptist Church (1892–93)

IUKA
First Baptist Church (1915)

JACKSON
Methodist Church (1838–39)
First Presbyterian Church (1843–46)
First Christian Church (circa 1845–50)
St. Peter's Catholic Church (1867–69)
St. Andrew's Episcopal Church (1869–73)
Temple Beth Israel (1874–75)
First Methodist Church (1883)
St. Columb's Chapel (Episcopal) (1892)
First Presbyterian Church (1892–93)
First Christian Church (1893)
First Baptist Church (1891–1900)
Griffith Memorial Baptist Church (1907)
First Church of Christ, Scientist (1911)
Seventh Day Adventist Church (circa 1915)
Temple Beth Israel (1940)

LAUREL
FirstPresbyterian Church (1901–2)
First Methodist Church (1912–13)
First Baptist Church (1920)

LONG BEACH
All Saints Episcopal Church (1895)

LOUISVILLE
Louisville Presbyterian Church (circa 1890)
First Baptist Church (1915)

MACON
First Baptist Church (1852)
Macon Presbyterian Church (1890)

MAGNOLIA
First Baptist Church (1895)
Magnolia Methodist Church (1898)

McCOMB
St. Alphonsus Catholic Church (1875–76)
First Baptist Church (1905)
Centenary Methodist Church (1906)
First Baptist Church (1923–24)

MERIDIAN
Temple Beth Israel (circa 1875)
Church of the Mediator (Episcopal) (1876–78)
Central Methodist Church (1885)
First Baptist Church (1892–93)
Temple Beth Israel (1906)

NATCHEZ VICINITY
Pine Ridge Presbyterian Church (1828)
Clear Creek Baptist Church (1828)

NEW ALBANY
First Baptist Church (1898–99)

NEWTON
First Methodist Church (circa 1900–4)
First Baptist Church (1908)

OXFORD
First Baptist Church (1881–82)

PASCAGOULA
First Presbyterian Church (1896)

PASS CHRISTIAN
Trinity Episcopal Church (circa 1849)
St. Paul's Catholic Church (1879)

PHILADELPHIA AND VICINITY
Carolina Presbyterian Church (1842)
First Baptist Church (1926)

PONTOTOC AND VICINITY
Zion Baptist Church
Toxish Baptist Church (1905)

PORT GIBSON AND VICINITY
"Old Magnolia Church" (circa 1845–50?)

RIPLEY
First Baptist Church (1916)

SCOOBA
Presbyterian Church (1890s?)

SENATOBIA
First Methodist Church (1880)

SHELBY
Shelby Methodist Church (1912)

STARKVILLE
First Presbyterian Church (1855)

VICKSBURG
Crawford Street Methodist Church (1846)
St. Paul's Catholic Church (circa 1850)
First Presbyterian Church (1855)
First Baptist Church (1878–79, 1906–7)
Bethel A.M.E. Church (1879)
Crawford Street Methodist Church (1899)

WATER VALLEY
Church of the Nativity (Episcopal) (circa 1895, 1918)

WEST POINT
First Baptist Church (1888)
Cumberland Presbyterian Church (1898)

YAZOO CITY
First Presbyterian Church (1887–88)
First Baptist Church (1904)
St. Stephen's Methodist Church (circa 1904)

Methodist Episcopal Church, South

Aberdeen, Monroe County (1859–60)

One of the finest Greek Revival churches built in Mississippi was the Methodist Episcopal Church (old First Methodist Church) in Aberdeen. Located at the northwest corner of West Quincy Street (now College Place) and North James Street, it was a rectangular brick building, elevated upon a raised basement and distinguished by an elegant monumental "distyle in muris" portico in the Grecian Ionic order. Construction began in 1859 and was completed in 1860. The first service was held on November 4, 1860.[1]

This handsome building was demolished about 1911 to make way for the construction of the present First United Methodist Church, which was built on the same site in 1912.[2]

The old First Baptist Church, Aberdeen.

First Baptist Church

Aberdeen, Monroe County (circa 1891–94)

The old First Baptist Church in Aberdeen was built sometime between 1891 and 1894 at the northeast corner of West Commerce and North Columbus streets. It was a brick building in the Romanesque Revival style with a diagonally projecting entrance tower at the southwestern front corner, and was very similar in appearance to the First Christian Church (1891–93), which stood nearby at the northwest corner of West Quincy Street (College Place) and North Hickory Street.

About 1927 the present sanctuary of First Baptist Church was built on the same site as the older building.

First Methodist Church
(Methodist Episcopal Church, South)

Amory, Monroe County (1914)

The old First Methodist Church (originally the Methodist Episcopal Church, South) in Amory was built in 1914. Located at the north corner of South Third Street and Second Avenue South (then called Walnut Street), it was a domed Neoclassical building of brick construction, with two identical front façades, each with a semi-recessed tetrastyle portico in the Roman Ionic order. This building was one of more than a dozen very similar Classical Revival churches in Mississippi sharing a distinctive diagonally symmetrical design that was curved around most of the rear, giving their plans a quarter-round shape. Other lost examples of this design were the old First Baptist Church in Columbia (1911–12) (see page 43), the old First Baptist Church in Cleveland (circa 1915–16), and the old First Baptist Church in Louisville (1915) (see page 126). Surviving church buildings of this same type include the First United Methodist Church in Batesville (1913) and First Baptist Church of Pontotoc (1914). Both of these buildings were designed by James E. Greene of Birmingham, Alabama,

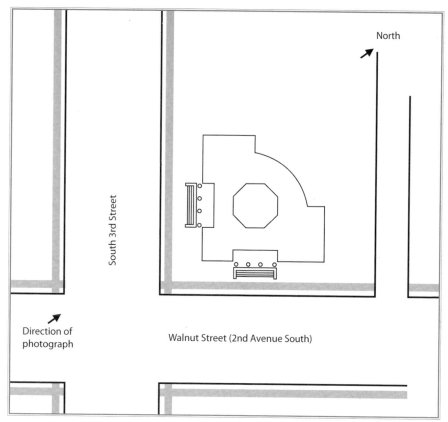

The site plan of the old First Methodist Church, Amory, showing the distinctive quarter-round shape.

suggesting that Greene was the architect of the Methodist church in Amory as well. Greene designed numerous other churches throughout the South during the 1910s and 1920s, including the old First Baptist Church in Orlando, Florida (1915). Among his other documented works in Mississippi, besides the churches with quarter-round plans, were the old First Baptist Church in Belzoni (1922) (see page 41) and the old First Baptist Church in Biloxi (1924) (see page 21), neither of which still stands.

The Methodist church in Amory burned in 1926 and was replaced on the same site by a new building, completed in 1927. On January 11, 1936, the replacement building also burned. It was rebuilt within the same walls later that year and stands today as First United Methodist Church.

First Baptist Church

Amory, Monroe County (1918)

Located on the north corner of Third Street and Maple Street, the old First Baptist Church of Amory, built in 1918, was a two-story Neoclassical brick building on a partially raised basement. The southwest main façade of the building was dominated by a semi-recessed portico with four unfluted Ionic columns. On the southeast secondary façade was a smaller portico consisting of two Ionic columns supporting an arch. The old First Baptist Church of Amory was virtually identical to the First Baptist Church in Sumner (1917–18), which still stands.

In 1960–61 a new sanctuary was built immediately adjacent to the old church, which continued to be used for several years thereafter as an education building until it was demolished in 1973.[3] A new education building has been built on its site.

"Church of Our Lady of the Gulf", Bay St. Louis, Miss. *M. M. Jaime*

Moore & Gibson Co., N.Y. *German* *the fever, I'm battled up here.*

Church of Our Lady of the Gulf (II)

Bay Saint Louis, Hancock County (1872)

The Catholic parish of Our Lady of the Gulf in Bay Saint Louis was established in 1847. The first church building was begun in 1848 and dedicated in 1849. In 1872 it was replaced by an impressive Gothic Revival church of brick construction. According to Sanborn fire insurance maps, the second church had a Latin cross plan with transepts extending to either side of the nave and a polygonal apse at the west end. At the east end, projecting from the center of the façade, facing the beach, was a massive tower surmounted by a tall, octagonal spire that was surely visible from a great distance in every direction.

This fine building was destroyed by a fire on November 15–16, 1907, and was subsequently replaced on the same site by the present Church of Our Lady of the Gulf.

First Baptist Church

Belzoni, Humphreys County (1922)

Another of the many churches in Mississippi designed by James E. Greene was the First Baptist Church in Belzoni, built in 1922. Located at 302 Pecan Street, at the southeast corner of Pecan Street and Central Avenue, it was a Neoclassical church with two semi-recessed tetrastyle porticos in the Roman Ionic order, one on the broader north façade and another on the narrower west façade. The auditorium was positioned above a full-story-height raised basement. Above the basement the walls had two-story fenestration, with round-arched windows on the lower story and flat-topped windows on the upper story.

A new sanctuary was later built immediately to the east of the old building, which was demolished soon thereafter.

Biloxi, Miss., Church in Biloxi that Jefferson Davis attended while residing at Beauvoir. Now Chapel of the Church of the Redeemer

Church of the Redeemer (Episcopal) (I)

Biloxi, Harrison County (1873–74)

The original building of the Church of the Redeemer (Episcopal) in Biloxi was built at the southwest corner of Water and Bellman streets in 1873–74. The regular worship services of the church were held in this building until 1891, when a newer church was completed just to the south, facing toward the Gulf of Mexico. After the completion of the new church, the older building became the chapel and parish hall, and served in this capacity for many years.

In 1969, Hurricane Camille destroyed the second church. The original building survived the storm, and was subsequently returned to use as a house of worship. The original Church of the Redeemer was listed on the National Register of Historic Places in 1984, along with the tower that was the only remnant of the second building.

When Hurricane Katrina devastated the Mississippi Gulf Coast on August 29, 2005, the first building of the Church of the Redeemer and the tower of the second building were both completely destroyed.

CHURCH OF THE REDEEMER, BILOXI, MISS.—15 JEFFERSON DAVIS WAS A VESTRYMAN OF THIS CHURCH

Church of the Redeemer (Episcopal) (II)

Biloxi, Harrison County (1891)

The second building of the Church of the Redeemer in Biloxi was erected in 1891. Located just south of the original building, the new church faced toward the Gulf of Mexico and the beachfront road that would later become Beach Boulevard. The architect was Thomas Sully, of the firm Sully & Toledano of New Orleans. After the second building was completed, the original church building, constructed in 1873–74, became the parish hall.

The second church was a charming combination of Gothic, Romanesque, and Shingle Style features. The lower walls of the building were brick. On the projecting wall across the front of the building were several small windows with Gothic pointed arches. The larger round-arched windows along the side walls rose above the line of the eaves of the roof and were sheltered by small gables. The main gable of the front façade and the upper half of the tower were clad in ornately patterned shingles. Within the gable were three tall, slender round-arched windows, and the doors at the base of the tower were round-arched. The church was surrounded by numerous large live oak trees, festooned with Spanish moss.

Interior of Historic Church of the Redeemer, Biloxi, Mississippi 134

16119

The interior of the second Church of the Redeemer, as shown on an old postcard.

Several postcards made in the early twentieth century, including the one depicted here, offer the comment that "Jefferson Davis was a vestryman of this church." Although that statement is true with regard to the church as an organization, it is incorrect in implying that Davis served as a vestryman in this building. Jefferson Davis never worshipped in this building, which was constructed three years after he died in December 1889. Davis attended services in the church that preceded this one, located just to the north, which became the parish hall after this second building was erected.

The picturesque location of the Church of the Redeemer, facing the waters of the Gulf of Mexico, became its downfall when Hurricane Camille struck the Gulf Coast on August 17, 1969. The hurricane destroyed the venerable building, leaving only its bell tower. After the storm, the tower was repaired to serve as a monument to those who died in Hurricane Camille, and the original 1874 church building was returned to use as a house of worship.

Although the original building and the tower of the second building had survived Hurricane Camille, they were unable to withstand the massive storm surge of Hurricane Katrina when it struck the Gulf Coast on August 29, 2005. Both structures were completely destroyed.

The bell tower of the second Church of the Redeemer remained standing after Hurricane Camille in 1969, and was repaired to serve as a memorial to those who died in the storm, but it was destroyed by Hurricane Katrina in 2005.

Main Street Methodist Church
(Methodist Episcopal Church, South)

Biloxi, Harrison County (1904–5)

The congregation now known as First United Methodist Church in Biloxi was formerly known as Main Street Methodist Episcopal Church, South. Its first permanent house of worship was a two-story wood-frame building, built in 1851, which also served for a time as the Masonic hall. In 1904 the cornerstone was laid for a second building at the same site, at the northeast corner of Main Street and Washington Street, facing south toward Washington Street.[4] Completed in 1905 and dedicated in 1908, it was a brick Romanesque Revival–style auditorium-plan church on a full-story raised basement.

The congregation worshiped in this building until about 1948. Soon thereafter they relocated to a new building, built in 1950, on Hopkins Boulevard. The old church was sold for commercial purposes and was later demolished.

In 2008, First United Methodist Church of Biloxi moved to a new location on Highway 67, north of Interstate 10.

The old First Baptist Church, Biloxi.

First Baptist Church

Biloxi, Harrison County (1924)

The former building of First Baptist Church of Biloxi, built in 1924, stood on the south side of Howard Avenue between Cuevas Street and Hopkins Boulevard, just west of Biloxi's downtown business district (and just east of where Interstate 110 was later built). The architect for this building was James E. Greene, and the contractor was F. B. Sarrell. This building replaced an earlier church, built in 1901, which had been located at the northeast corner of Lameuse Street and Washington Street.

The old First Baptist Church of Biloxi was a Neoclassical building with two-story fenestration, on a full-story raised brick basement, with a very shallow two-story-height monumental false portico[5] in the Ionic order. The portico did not shelter the entrances, which were located to either side. This plan form, with entrances in the corners flanking a center false portico, was a widely used plan for Neoclassical churches during the 1920s. The larger churches of this type had, like the First Baptist Church in Biloxi, a hexastyle (six-column) portico. Another lost church with this basic form in Mississippi was the old First Baptist Church in McComb (1923–24) (see page 138). The present building of First Baptist Church of New Albany (1923–24) is a surviving example. First Baptist Church in Philadelphia (1926) (see page 163) exemplified a smaller version of this basic form which had a tetrastyle (four-column) portico.

After the congregation of First Baptist Church of Biloxi relocated to a large new facility near Interstate 10 in the late 1990s, the 1924 sanctuary was sold to Beau Rivage Casino. The old church was demolished in January 2001 to create more parking for the casino.

First Methodist Church
(Methodist Episcopal Church, South)

Booneville, Prentiss County (1897)

Built in 1897, the old First Methodist Church (Methodist Episcopal Church, South) in Booneville stood at the north corner of Main Street and Church Street, directly across Main Street from the Prentiss County Courthouse. The church was very similar in its detailing to the old First Baptist Church of New Albany (1898–99) (see page 150), and was probably constructed by the same builder. The design of this building appears to be adapted from one of the mail-order church plans of Benjamin D. Price.[6]

About 1928 the congregation relocated to a new building at 400 West Church Street,[7] and the old church was subsequently demolished. In 1939 a post office was built on the site.

Perspective No. 220. Price, $150.00. Brick.

Extreme dimensions, 66 x 102 feet; auditorium contains 450 seats; choir and organ in rear of pulpit; lecture room, 31 x 40 feet, 240 chairs; infant class room is 12 x 28 feet; one class room is 12 x 16 feet; four class rooms, each 9½ x 16 feet; study 12 x 12 feet; library, 7 x 12 feet; rooms connect by folding doors and rolling partitions; heated by steam; walls are 20 feet; ceiling of lecture room, 26 feet; ceiling of auditorium, 33 feet high; rafters partially exposed; ceiling decorated with wood work; bowled floor; small tower is 55 feet high; large tower is 12 x 12 feet, 90 feet high.

Approximate cost, $16,000.

105

Like the old First Presbyterian Church in Corinth, the design of the old First Methodist Church in Booneville appears to have been adapted from the Benjamin Price plan that was shown as Perspective No. #220 in *Church Plans* (1906). The education wing shown on the plan (labeled as "lecture room") was omitted from the design of the church in Booneville.

Brandon Methodist Church in the late 1930s.

Brandon Methodist Church
(Methodist Episcopal Church, South)

Brandon, Rankin County (1867–73)

Brandon Methodist Church was organized in 1836. Its first building was burned by Union troops during the Civil War. After the war it was replaced by a substantial brick church in the Romanesque Revival style at the location of the present church. Begun in 1867 and completed in 1873, it was distinguished by a slightly projecting center front tower surmounted by a tall octagonal spire. This church was unusual in that its tower was flanked by twin entrances, set within round-arched openings. Center front towers were typical of Romanesque Revival churches of the 1860s and 1870s, but they normally contained a single center entrance, instead of being flanked by paired entrances.

The second building of Brandon Methodist Church was demolished in April 1958 to allow for the construction of a new sanctuary that was built on the same site later that year.

First Methodist Church
(Methodist Episcopal Church, South)

Brookhaven, Lincoln County (1904)

The second building of First Methodist Church in Brookhaven stood on the north side of West Cherokee Street just west of Church Street, adjacent to Whitworth College. It was a Gothic style auditorium-plan church built in 1904. It was evidently constructed from plans prepared by Benjamin D. Price, of Atlantic Highlands, New Jersey, who provided mail-order plans for hundreds of churches throughout the United States, including over forty churches in Mississippi.

This building was virtually identical to the old Methodist churches in Kinsley, Kansas, and New Bethlehem, Pennsylvania, which no longer stand. A surviving example of this design is the First United Methodist Church in Hinton, West Virginia.

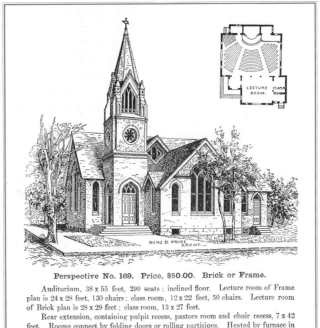

Perspective No. 169. Price, $50.00. Brick or Frame.

Auditorium, 38 x 55 feet, 290 seats ; inclined floor. Lecture room of Frame plan is 24 x 28 feet, 130 chairs ; class room, 12 x 22 feet, 50 chairs. Lecture room of Brick plan is 28 x 29 feet ; class room, 13 x 27 feet.

Rear extension, containing pulpit recess, pastors room and choir recess, 7 x 42 feet. Rooms connect by folding doors or rolling partitions. Heated by furnace in cellar ; walls, 16 feet : ceiling, 29 feet high, decorated with wood work ; tower, 12 x 12 feet, 70 feet high.

Approximate cost, $5000 to $7000.

The Methodist Church in Brookhaven was almost identical to the design pictured as Perspective No. 169 in *Church Plans*, a catalog of designs by Benjamin D. Price and Max Charles Price published in 1906.

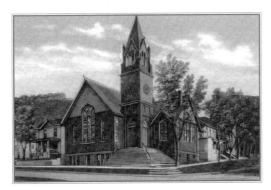

First Methodist Church, Hinton, West Virginia.

The old Methodist Church, Kinsley, Kansas.

The congregation grew so rapidly after this building was completed that within only a dozen years a much larger building was needed.[8] The old church was replaced by the present building, a handsome Neoclassical edifice constructed across Cherokee Street in 1916–17.[9] The old building was apparently demolished soon thereafter.

The Mail-Order Church Plans
of Benjamin D. Price

It has become widely known that from the 1880s to the 1910s many private homes were built from plans purchased by mail order. Particularly prominent among the architects who sold mail-order house plans was George Barber of Knoxville, Tennessee. The subject of mail-order house plans has received much attention in recent years, and several books have been written on the subject. It is not as well known, however, that during the same period numerous churches were also built with the use of mail-order plans, and there were architects who specialized in mail-order church plans.

One of the most prolific of the designers of mail-order church plans during this period was Benjamin D. Price. Originally from Philadelphia, Pennsylvania, Price later relocated to Atlantic Highlands, New Jersey, where he and his son Max Charles Price did an extensive trade in church plans. These plans were advertised through catalogs that were compiled annually. Hundreds of churches all across the United States were built from plans prepared by Benjamin Price. Price's plans were promoted extensively by the Boards of Church Extension of the Methodist Episcopal Church and the Methodist Episcopal Church, South (which were separate denominations at the time), so a large proportion of Price churches are Methodist, but they were also widely adopted for churches of other denominations, including Baptist, Presbyterian, Christian (Disciples of Christ), and African Methodist Episcopal (A.M.E.) congregations.

Price's mail-order plans were especially popular for small, newly organized, financially challenged congregations that were being established by the hundreds or even thousands in the towns and villages that were springing up throughout the country along America's rapidly expanding railroad network. Small wooden churches could be built very economically in these communities with inexpensive and readily available lumber. In Mississippi, wooden churches of this type were built throughout the state, particularly in railroad towns and lumber-mill towns.

At least forty churches in Mississippi are believed to have been built either directly from Benjamin Price plans or from local builders' adaptations of his plans. Some of these still stand retaining their original designs, including Main Street United Methodist Church in Bay St. Louis, the United Methodist Church at Black Hawk in Carroll County, New Hebron United Methodist Church, First United Methodist Church in Poplarville, and the old First Methodist Church

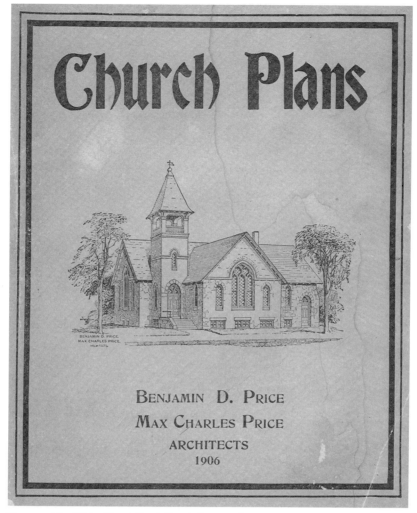

Church Plans

BENJAMIN D. PRICE

MAX CHARLES PRICE

ARCHITECTS

1906

The cover of the 1906 edition of *Church Plans* by Benjamin D. Price and Max Charles Price. This was the thirty-first annual edition of the plan catalog.

(now First Christian Church) in West Point. Some other churches built from Price plans still stand, but have undergone alterations, such as Zion Chapel A.M.E. Church in Hattiesburg and St. Peter A.M.E. Church in Port Gibson, which have been clad in brick veneer. But many churches that were built in Mississippi from plans devised by Benjamin Price no longer survive. Among these were the old First Methodist Church in Brookhaven, the old Louisville Presbyterian Church, the old Presbyterian Church in Scooba, and numerous others. Other lost churches that were probably adapted from Price plans included the old First Methodist Church in Booneville, the old First Presbyterian Church in Corinth, and the old First Baptist Church in New Albany.

Presbyterian Church (later Baptist Church)

Buena Vista, Chickasaw County (1860)

This building, which stood for many years in the rural community of Buena Vista, east of Houston in the southeastern part of Chickasaw County, was originally built about 1860 as the Presbyterian Church, and it served as such until about 1913. Thereafter it served as the Baptist Church from 1913 until 1933.[10]

It was a simple vernacular church of wood-frame construction with modest Greek Revival features, such as the design of the front gable in the form of a classical pediment and detailing of the corner-boards as classical pilasters. The twin front entrances were double-leaf doors of a Greek Revival design, topped by rectangular transoms.

The fenestration (the arrangement of windows) makes the building appear to contain two stories, but that can be misleading, because among the several widely used building forms that were typical of vernacular churches in Mississippi in the nineteenth century, there were two different building forms that ordinarily had two tiers of windows, and these two forms were in many cases indistinguishable from each other when viewed from the outside. One of these typical forms contained two separate stories, each with its own set of windows, and the upper story typically was used as a fraternal lodge hall. Another typical form of vernacular church building contained a single large preaching hall that was two stories in height, and contained an interior gallery or balcony that was illuminated by the upper tier of windows. It cannot be determined, simply from looking at the photograph of the exterior of the Buena Vista church, whether it contained an open preaching hall or whether it contained two separate stories. In the photograph, however, one can see that the shutters are closed over all of the upper-tier windows, which suggests that the building probably had two separate stories. If so, the upper story might have been the meeting place of the local Masonic lodge, Pikeville Lodge No. 85, which moved to Buena Vista from Pikeville in 1859 and became inactive about 1935.

The Buena Vista church was photographed for the WPA sometime between 1936 and 1940, but it was destroyed not long after that.

The old Presbyterian Church, Canton.

Presbyterian Church

Canton, Madison County (1852–53)

The old Presbyterian Church in Canton was a rectangular brick building with Greek Revival features, similar to the original Christian Church in Jackson (see page 96). Built in 1852–53,[11] it stood at the southeast corner of Peace Street and Priestley Street, facing north toward Peace Street. It was replaced by the present First Presbyterian Church, which was constructed on the same site in 1922.

Temple B'nai Israel

Canton, Madison County (1877)

Canton's Jewish congregation was organized in 1873.[12] In 1877, a synagogue named Temple B'nai Israel was built at the northeast corner of South Liberty Street and East Academy Street.[13] This location was directly across Liberty Street from the old Methodist Church (which was where the present sanctuary of First United Methodist Church would be built in 1922).[14] The synagogue was a small, modest, rectangular wooden building with eclectic Late Victorian Italianate and Stick Style features.

The Temple B'nai Israel building had ceased to be used for regular services by about 1971.[15] It had stood for almost a century before it was demolished in 1975.[16] Its site is now part of the Breeland Funeral Home complex.

First Methodist Church
(Methodist Episcopal Church, South)

Clarksdale, Coahoma County (1897)

The second building of the First Methodist Church (originally the Methodist Episcopal Church, South) of Clarksdale, erected in 1897, was located at the northeast corner of Leflore Avenue and Second Street. A wood-frame Gothic Revival building with a prominent front corner tower, it was identical to the old First Baptist Church (no longer extant) in Dade City, Florida, which indicates that it was built from a mail-order plan. The tower was also similar to the one on the old Methodist Church in Edwards, Mississippi, constructed in 1899 (see page 62).

The designer of these buildings has not been documented, but the similarity of those towers to the tower of the church shown as Design K by the Denver,

The old First Baptist Church in Dade City, Florida, was identical to the old First Methodist Church in Clarksdale, indicating that they were built from the same plans.

PERSPECTIVE VIEW.

The tower of the old First Methodist Church in Clarksdale was very similar to the tower of Design K by F. E. Kidder as depicted on plate XXXIV in his *Churches and Chapels*, published in 1900.

Colorado, architect F. E. Kidder, in his book *Churches and Chapels*, published in 1900, suggests that Kidder may have prepared the original mail-order plans for all three of these churches.

In 1917 the old First Methodist Church in Clarksdale was replaced by the present sanctuary on the same site.

First Presbyterian Church

Clarksdale, Coahoma County (circa 1915–17)

The second building of First Presbyterian Church in Clarksdale stood at the northwest corner of Second Street and Sharkey Avenue. Designed by Charles O. Pfeil of Memphis, it was built circa 1915–17, replacing an earlier wooden church that had stood on the same site.

This church was a brick building, surmounted by a ribbed dome that was set upon an octagonal drum. The entrances were located at the corners. It was somewhat unusual among Classical Revival churches of the time in that it did not have a portico; instead, there were pedimented sections of the walls, embellished by pilasters, projecting slightly from the center of each façade, which gave the visual suggestion of porticos.

First Presbyterian Church later relocated to 900 West Second Street, and this building was subsequently demolished.

First Christian Church (Disciples of Christ)

Clarksdale, Coahoma County (1923–29)

The old First Christian Church in Clarksdale stood at the southwest corner of Leflore Avenue and First Street. The building was built in two stages. The first stage was the construction of the basement, which was built in 1923 and was given a temporary roof so that the congregation could begin meeting there. The Sanborn fire insurance map of Clarksdale prepared in May 1923 shows an outline of the building with the notations "TO BE CHURCH" and "COV'D CONC. FOUND'N" (covered concrete foundation). The second stage of construction was completed several years later, and the building was dedicated on May 3, 1929.[17] The completed building appears on the Sanborn map of 1929.

The architect of the building is not documented, but it seems likely to have been Raymond B. Spencer (1887–1959), an Iowa native who was working in

Memphis in the 1920s. He was a partner in the firm of Spencer & Abbott, who designed Clarksdale Baptist Church, built in 1919–20.[18] Spencer also designed the First Baptist Church in Leland (1922–23)[19], which has similar detailing to the Christian Church.

According to an article that appeared in the *Clarksdale Press Register* in 1982, "In October 1973, after the First Christian Church congregation had built a new church on DeSoto Street extended, the building on Leflore was sold to the Episcopal congregation, whose church is situated across an alley to the west. The Episcopal group apparently considered expanding their facilities into the former Christian Church but then decided to dispose of the property."[20] In 1982 the property was sold to the Federal Land Bank Association of Cleveland, who demolished the building later that year in order to construct an office building on the site.

Baptist Church

Collins, Covington County (1925)

Not all Neoclassical churches from the 1920s were large monumental buildings. Many that were built in small towns and rural areas were modest in size and architectural character, such as the second building of the Baptist Church at Collins, which was built in 1925, replacing an earlier building that had been erected in 1905.[21] Located at the north corner of Fourth Street and Avenue D,[22] it was a temple-form brick church with a tetrastyle portico, elevated atop a partially raised basement story. The church was similar in appearance to some of the Greek Revival churches of the 1840s and 1850s, such as College Hill Presbyterian Church in Lafayette County, built in 1846.[23]

The second building of Collins Baptist Church was replaced by the present, third building in 1950.

The old First Baptist Church, Columbia.

First Baptist Church

Columbia, Marion County (1911–12)

Like the old First Methodist Church in Amory (see page 10) and the old Baptist Church in Louisville (see page 126), the old First Baptist Church of Columbia was among the several Neoclassical churches in Mississippi with a diagonally symmetrical quarter-round plan. Similar to most of the other churches of this type, it was a two-story brick building on a raised basement, with two perpendicularly adjacent front façades. Each façade contained a semi-recessed two-story-height tetrastyle portico. Most of the back wall, which extended around the north and west sides of the building, was curved, giving the building its distinctive quarter-round floor plan. Atop the center of the building was a dome.

Built in 1911–12,[24] the old First Baptist Church stood at the northeast corner of High School Avenue and Dale Street. Although the name of the architect has not been documented, the building was almost certainly designed by J.E. Greene of Birmingham, Alabama, who is known to have designed several of the churches that have this particular plan and appearance. Surviving examples of the type include the First United Methodist Church in Batesville (1913) and the First Baptist Church in Pontotoc (1914), both of which are documented to have been designed by Greene.

In 1961 the present sanctuary of First Baptist Church was built immediately to the east of the old church, which was later demolished. The site of the old building is now a grassy lawn.

First Baptist Church, Columbus, Miss.

First Baptist Church

Columbus, Lowndes County (1838–40)

The old First Baptist Church in Columbus, begun in 1838 and completed in 1840, was an exceptionally fine early Greek Revival church. At the time of its construction it must have been the most elegant house of worship in Mississippi and one of the largest and finest Baptist churches in the South. It was contemporary with such other notable Greek Revival churches as Christ Episcopal Church in Mobile, Alabama (1838–41) and Christ Episcopal Church in Savannah, Georgia (1837–38), and it predated St. Paul's Episcopal Church in Richmond, Virginia (1844–45) and Tabb Street Presbyterian Church in Petersburg, Virginia (1843).

Located at the northeast corner of Seventh Street North (originally Caledonia Street) and First Avenue North (originally Military Street), facing westward, it was a rectangular temple-form building of brick construction, with an integral tetrastyle portico in the Grecian Ionic order with elegant fluted columns. The building was surmounted by an unusual steeple made of five octagonal drums descending in size in each successive tier but remaining consistent in proportion. This steeple was clearly inspired by the five-tier octagonal spire that Sir

First Baptist Church, Columbus, as pictured in *Art Work of Mississippi* in 1901.

Christopher Wren placed atop the tower of St. Bride's Church, Fleet Street, in London (1671–78).[25] From the arrangement of the windows, the building appears to have had a split-level interior, arranged so that the entrance from the portico (reached by a short, broad flight of steps) opened to a vestibule at the same level, from which stairs led up to the elevated auditorium and probably also down to the full-story basement.

Built at the same time that the Old State Capitol was being constructed in Jackson, the old First Baptist Church in Columbus was similar in appearance to the Lyceum at the University of Mississippi (1846–48) and the Male and Female Academy at Lexington (circa 1850), both designed by William Nichols, the

The Lyceum at the University of Mississippi, designed by William Nichols.

architect of the Old Capitol. The similarity to those buildings and the fact that Nichols was one of the very few architects in the state at the time with sufficient skill to design such a building suggest that William Nichols could have been the architect.

This remarkable building was evidently demolished about 1905 in order to make room for the construction of the present First Baptist Church, a Gothic Revival auditorium-plan church which was constructed in 1908.[26]

Greek Revival Churches, 1838–1860

Given that Mississippi has such a wealth of fine white-columned antebellum residences in the Greek Revival style, it may seem surprising that there are so few Greek Revival churches. The reason is that, prior to the Civil War and for a long time afterwards, Mississippi was a predominantly rural state, with few large towns and no cities comparable in size to Richmond, Charleston, Savannah, Mobile, or New Orleans. It was in these great cites of the South that most of the region's finest Greek Revival churches and synagogues were built—such buildings as Government Street Presbyterian Church in Mobile (1836–37), Christ Church in Savannah (1837–38), Beth Elohim Synagogue in Charleston (1840–41), and St. Paul's Episcopal Church in Richmond (1844–45). Several very fine Greek Revival churches were built in Mississippi, but few of these still stand. Rare surviving examples include Trinity Episcopal Church in Natchez (as remodeled in 1838), Oakland Chapel at Alcorn State University (1840–51), the former Second Presbyterian Church (now Zion A.M.E. Church) in Natchez (1858), and Provine Chapel at Mississippi College in Clinton (1859). Smaller rural examples include College Hill Presbyterian Church near Oxford (1846) and Kingston Methodist Church near Natchez (1856–57).

Mississippi had several other particularly notable Greek Revival churches that no longer survive. The most impressive of these were First Baptist Church in Columbus (1838–40) and First Methodist Church in Aberdeen (1859–60). Other smaller Greek Revival churches included Bethel Presbyterian Church near Columbus (1844–45), the Baptist Church in Macon (1852), and the Presbyterian Church in Starkville (1855).

Bethel Presbyterian Church

South of Columbus, Lowndes County (1844–45)

Located in rural Lowndes County, about twelve miles south of Columbus, Bethel Presbyterian Church, built in 1844–45, was a small but elegantly proportioned Greek Revival church of wood-frame construction, distinguished architecturally by a distyle-in-muris portico.[27] This type of portico was a popular motif in Greek Revival architecture, appearing in the designs of such notable Greek Revival churches as Government Street Presbyterian Church in Mobile (1836–37), Christ Church in Mobile (1838–41), and Trinity Methodist Church in Savannah (1848–50).[28] The old Methodist Church in Aberdeen, Mississippi (1859–60), (see page 7) also featured a distyle-in-muris portico. A surviving example in Mississippi is the old Baptist Church in Jackson (1843–44). The form appeared in other small rural churches as well, such as Robinson Springs Methodist Church in Elmore County, Alabama (1845).

Bethel Presbyterian Church was destroyed by a tornado on November 10, 2002. Its site is marked by a state historical marker.

Robinson Springs Methodist Church, in Elmore County, Alabama, built in 1845.

The ruins of Bethel Presbyterian Church following its destruction by a tornado on November 10, 2002.

(Old) First Methodist Church
(First Methodist Episcopal Church, South)

Corinth, Alcorn County (1890–92, enlarged and remodeled 1905–6)

The old First Methodist Church in Corinth was located at 514 Taylor Street, at the southeast corner of Taylor and Foote streets, facing west toward the court-house square. It was just north of the Waldron Hotel, on the same block. As originally built in 1890–92, it was a cruciform brick church with transepts extending to the sides and a projecting vestibule at the center of the front façade. In 1905–6 the building was substantially remodeled and enlarged.[29] The architect for the remodeling was Reuben A. Heavner of Jackson, Tennessee, and the contractor was A. H. Patrick.[30] The remodeling widened the building considerably on the south side, probably converting it to an auditorium plan, and added two corner towers to the front façade. The remodeling was so extensive that the building was given a new cornerstone, inscribed with the date 1905, which gives the impression that the structure was completely rebuilt; however, a careful examination of old photos and the outline of the building as shown on Sanborn fire insurance maps indicates that parts of the earlier building were retained in the remodeling.

The old church was demolished about 1961, after the congregation relocated to its present building at 901 Fillmore Street in 1960.

First Methodist Church, Corinth, as it appeared in the late 1930s.

First Baptist Church

Corinth, Alcorn County (1894–95, remodeled 1912–14)

Not all "lost" church buildings are completely gone. Some, like the third building of First Baptist Church of Corinth, are still partially extant, but they have been converted to other uses and have been so extensively remodeled that they are no longer recognizable.

This church stood at the southeast corner of Fillmore and Childs streets, facing westward toward Fillmore Street. It was originally built in 1894–95, and was dedicated on June 26, 1898.[31] The building was extensively remodeled and enlarged from September 1912 to April 1914 by A. H. Patrick, contractor.[32] As originally built, it was a Romanesque Revival building with a broach spire on its northwest corner tower, but when the church was enlarged and remodeled the

First Baptist Church, Corinth, in the late 1930s, after having been extensively remodeled from 1912 to 1914.

Remnants of the old First Baptist Church, Corinth, in 2008, behind a commercial façade.

building was given a more Italian Romanesque styling, and the corner tower was given the character of an Italian Romanesque campanile.

It is thought that Reuben Harrison Hunt of Chattanooga, Tennessee, may have designed the church, but the building in its original form did not resemble any of his other designs, and it seems more likely that he was the architect for the remodeling, rather than for the original construction.[33]

The building ceased to be used as a church about 1951, after the congregation relocated to the present First Baptist Church building on Main Street at the north end of Fillmore Street. The old church was later extensively remodeled to convert it to a commercial building, and is no longer recognizable from the front, but the side and rear walls of the church building can still be seen.

First Presbyterian Church

Corinth, Alcorn County (1894–96)

The old First Presbyterian Church of Corinth stood at the northeast corner of Foote and Franklin streets, across Foote Street from the north side of the courthouse square. It was begun in 1894 and completed in 1896. The architect is reported to have been A. J. Callahan,[34] but the design of the building appears to

Perspective No. 220. Price, $150.00. Brick.

Extreme dimensions, 66 x 102 feet; auditorium contains 450 seats; choir and organ in rear of pulpit; lecture room, 31 x 40 feet, 240 chairs; infant class room is 12 x 28 feet; one class room is 12 x 16 feet; four class rooms, each 9½ x 16 feet; study 12 x 12 feet; library, 7 x 12 feet; rooms connect by folding doors and rolling partitions; heated by steam; walls are 20 feet; ceiling of lecture room, 26 feet; ceiling of auditorium, 33 feet high; rafters partially exposed; ceiling decorated with wood work; bowled floor; small tower is 55 feet high; large tower is 12 x 12 feet, 90 feet high.

Approximate cost, $16,000.

105

This plan, shown as Perspective No. 220 in the thirty-first annual edition of *Church Plans* by Benjamin D. Price and Max Charles Price, published in 1906, was apparently the source of the design of the old First Presbyterian Church of Corinth.

have been based upon a mail-order plan prepared by Benjamin D. Price, architect, of Atlantic Highlands, New Jersey,[35] so perhaps Callahan was either the contractor or the supervising architect, executing (and perhaps modifying) a plan originally prepared by Price.

In 1949 the congregation purchased land on Shiloh Road, intending to build a new church complex there. A new education building and fellowship hall were completed at the new location at 919 East Shiloh Road in 1952,[36] and the congregation evidently moved to the facility at that time. The present sanctuary was completed there in 1957. The old church was apparently demolished by late 1955, and a JC Penney store was built on the site, opening on April 5, 1956.

The old First Presbyterian Church, Corinth, as pictured on an early postcard.

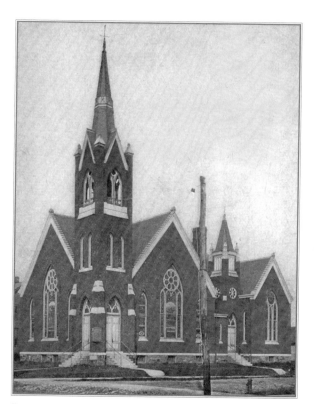

The old First Presbyterian Church of Berwick, Pennsylvania, which was clearly built from the design shown as Perspective No. 220, was similar in appearance to the First Presbyterian Church of Corinth.

Crystal Springs United Methodist Church as it appeared in June 1996.

Crystal Springs United Methodist Church was almost identical in appearance to Dresden United Methodist Church in Dresden, Tennessee, shown here.

Crystal Springs Methodist Church
(Methodist Episcopal Church, South)

Crystal Springs, Copiah County (1919)

Built in 1919 at 306 West Georgetown Street, the old Crystal Springs United Methodist Church was a Neoclassical building of brick construction, elevated upon a partially raised basement, with a shallow projecting hexastyle (six-column) portico in the Corinthian order. It was nearly identical in appearance to the First Methodist Church in Tallassee, Alabama (circa 1920–25), the First Methodist Church in Dresden, Tennessee (1923), and the old First Methodist Church (now an arts center) in Canton, Georgia (1925–26). The architectural prominence of the building had been recognized in 1997 by its inclusion in the National Register of Historic Places as a contributing component of the Crystal Springs Historic District.

Inclusion in a National Register historic district was not enough to spare the building from destruction, however. It was demolished in May 1999 to make room for the construction of a new sanctuary on the same site.

Drew Baptist Church

Drew, Sunflower County (1920)

Built in 1920, the old Drew Baptist Church stood at the southwest corner of Church Street and Prentiss Street. It was apparently the second building constructed for a congregation that had been founded in 1900. The architect has not been identified but may have been James E. Greene. The building was similar to several other Baptist churches built about the same time, so it seems likely that the plans were provided by the Architectural Department of the Baptist Sunday School Board.

This church was a brick building on a raised basement, with a semi-recessed tetrastyle portico in the Roman Ionic order. The walls had two-story fenestration with detailing similar to that of the First Baptist Church in Columbia. The old First Baptist Church in Monroeville, Alabama, was also very similar in appearance.

The old Drew Baptist Church was destroyed by fire on December 19, 1955.[37]

First Baptist Church

Durant, Holmes County (1898)

The First Baptist Church in Durant was organized in 1867. Its second sanctuary, shown here, was erected in 1898.[38] It was a Gothic Revival brick building located at the southwest corner of Mulberry and West streets. The design appears to be based on or adapted from a plan by Benjamin D. Price.[39]

In 1940–41 it was replaced by the present building at the same location.

Edwards Methodist Church
(Methodist Episcopal Church, South)

Edwards, Hinds County (1899)

The third building of Edwards Methodist Church was located at 211 Magnolia Street, at the southeast corner of Magnolia and Church streets. Built in 1899, it was a wood-frame Carpenter Gothic church with Shingle Style features. Its broad, shingle-clad arched porches were particularly distinctive. The front corner tower was very similar to that of the old First Methodist Church of Clarksdale (1897) (see page 35), suggesting that both buildings were designed by the same architect, possibly F. E. Kidder.

The building burned in 1938. The Sanborn fire insurance map of March 1938 shows a vacant lot where the church had been located. The present sanctuary of Edwards United Methodist Church was later built on the same site.

St. James Episcopal Church

Greenville, Washington County (1885–86; enlarged 1895)

The old St. James Episcopal Church in Greenville was a wood-frame eclectic Gothic Revival building located at the east corner of Washington Avenue and Broadway. The cornerstone was laid on June 1, 1885, and the completed building was consecrated on March 13, 1887. It was substantially enlarged in 1895. As originally constructed, the building apparently consisted of what later became the transverse portion at the rear of the building, which was a rectangular structure with an attached tower, essentially identical in form and detailing to St. James Episcopal Church in Port Gibson, except built of wood instead of brick.[40] The design can, therefore, be attributed to W. P. Wentworth of Boston, Massachusetts, who was the architect of the church in Port Gibson.

The enlargement in 1895 consisted of the addition of a new nave, attached perpendicularly to the original structure. At the southwest end of the nave, facing Washington Avenue, was a triple-gabled porch with spindlework detailing.

St. James Episcopal Church in Port Gibson (1884–85), before it was enlarged about 1897, was almost identical to the northwestern transept of St. James Episcopal Church in Greenville, except that its walls were built of brick.

The church was distinguished by having three towers, one over the center crossing and one on each transept. In 1919–20 the building was remodeled and was clad in a brick veneer.[41]

The old church was demolished in 1951 after the congregation moved to a new building at 1026 South Washington Avenue.[42]

First Presbyterian Church

Greenville, Washington County (1901–2)

The third building of First Presbyterian Church of Greenville was an auditorium-plan church of brick construction located at the north corner of Washington Avenue and Theobald Street. Begun in 1901, it was dedicated on June 22, 1902.[43] A Sunday school annex was added to the northeastern end of the building sometime before 1911.

In 1951 the congregation moved to a new church complex at 1 John Calvin Circle, off Goldstein Street east of South Main near the Greenville Cemetery. The old building was demolished soon thereafter.

Methodist Church of Greenville, Miss.

First Methodist Church
(Methodist Episcopal Church, South)

Greenville, Washington County (1903–4)

The fourth building constructed for the First Methodist Church in Greenville was a Romanesque Revival auditorium-plan church that stood at the northwest corner of Washington Avenue and North Shelby Street. The cornerstone was laid on June 24, 1903,[44] and the building was dedicated in 1904.[45] Although the architect has not yet been identified, the building is very similar in its form and detailing to the Methodist Church in Front Royal, Virginia, built in 1904, which was designed by Benjamin D. Price.

The old church was replaced on the same site by the present sanctuary of First United Methodist Church, which was begun in 1949 and completed in 1950.[46]

First Methodist Church, Greenville, in the 1930s.

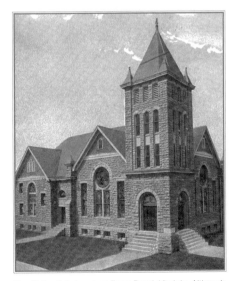

The Methodist church at Front Royal, Virginia. Although built of stone instead of brick, it has the same overall form and fenestration as the old First Methodist Church in Greenville.

Neo-medieval Auditorium-Plan Churches

The 1880s saw the introduction of a new architectural form for American churches. Combining an exterior appearance derived from traditional religious architecture with an internal configuration derived from the architecture of theaters, this new form, called the "auditorium church" or "auditorium-plan church," was designed to provide an optimal setting for preaching. The auditorium-plan church is distinguished by a worship space that consists of a wide auditorium with a floor that slopes downward toward a raised pulpit platform and with seating arranged in concentric curving arcs. In most cases the seating is in the form of curved pews, but in a few rare cases curved rows of individual folding theater seats are used (as at First Presbyterian Church in Yazoo City). In many cases the main axis of this curved seating is set on a diagonal to the main axis of the building, though in other cases the seating is arranged on the main center axis.

From the late 1880s through the early decades of the twentieth century, the auditorium-plan church enjoyed great popularity in Mississippi, and many buildings of this type were built throughout the state, particularly for Baptist, Methodist, and Presbyterian congregations. During the 1890s and early 1900s, auditorium-plan churches were typically designed in one of the two Neo-medieval styles—either the Gothic Revival or Romanesque Revival style. A few churches, such as Centenary Methodist Church in McComb (1906) (see page 137), combined elements of both styles. Some Neo-medieval auditorium churches continued to be built through the 1910s and into the early 1920s, though during this period Neoclassical designs became increasingly popular.

Many of the finest auditorium-plan churches in Mississippi (and indeed throughout the South) were designed by Reuben Harrison Hunt of Chattanooga, Tennessee. During the 1890s and early 1900s many of Hunt's auditorium churches were designed in the Romanesque Revival style. Surviving examples include First United Methodist Church in Greenwood (1898), Moore Memorial United Methodist Church in Winona (1898), First Presbyterian Church in Vicksburg (1906–8), Bay Street Presbyterian Church in Hattiesburg (1907–8), and First United Methodist Church in Pontotoc (1910).

Romanesque auditorium-plan churches by R. H. Hunt that no longer survive included the First Presbyterian Church in Jackson (1891–92), Hazlehurst Baptist Church (1892), and First Baptist Church in Meridian (1892–93). The First Baptist Church in Hattiesburg (1900–1) may also have been designed by Hunt. Nonextant Romanesque auditorium-plan churches by other (or unidentified) architects include First Baptist Church in Jackson (1891–99), First Christian

Church in Jackson (1893), the Presbyterian Church in West Point (1898), First Methodist Church in Greenville (1903–4), First Baptist Church in Yazoo City (1904), and Main Street Methodist Church in Biloxi (1904–5).

Auditorium-plan churches in the Gothic Revival style designed by R. H. Hunt include First Baptist Church in Columbus (1908) and First United Methodist Church in Aberdeen (1912). Other surviving Gothic Revival auditorium churches in Mississippi are First Presbyterian Church in Grenada (1905), Cleveland Street Associate Reformed Presbyterian Church in New Albany (1905), First Presbyterian Church in Yazoo City (1905–6), First Presbyterian Church in Brookhaven (1906–7), First United Methodist Church in Yazoo City (1907), First Baptist Church in Macon (1909), Main Street United Methodist Church in Hattiesburg (1907–10), First Presbyterian Church in Meridian (1912), and J. J. White Memorial Presbyterian Church in McComb (1921).

Lost examples include First Baptist Church in Grenada (1888), First Baptist Church in Durant (1898), Crawford Street Methodist Church in Vicksburg (1899), First Presbyterian Church in Greenville (1901–2), First Baptist Church in McComb (1905), First Baptist Church in Greenville, (1906–7), and First Baptist Church in Laurel (1920).

Adapted from "Religious Architecture in Mississippi from the 1820s through the 1920s" in *Historic Churches of Mississippi.*

Baptist Church, Greenville, Miss.

First Baptist Church

Greenville, Washington County (1906–07)

Begun in 1906 and completed in 1907, the old First Baptist Church of Greenville was a Gothic Revival auditorium-plan church with curved seating arranged on a diagonal axis. It was located at 411 Main Street, on the southwest corner of Main Street and Hinds Street, where the present sanctuary now stands.

The architect has not been documented, but the building was very similar to the Methodist Church built in 1908–9 at Pleasant Ridge, Ohio (a suburb of Cincinnati),[47] which was designed by Charles Crapsey, a Cincinnati architect who specialized in religious architecture and designed many churches throughout the United States, predominantly in the midwestern states.[48] Among the other churches he designed were the First Methodist Church in London, Ohio (1894), the former First Presbyterian Church in Parkersburg, West Virginia (1895), and the First Presbyterian Church in Bloomington, Indiana (1901), all of which are still extant.

The old sanctuary of First Baptist Church was demolished in 1953 to allow for the construction of the present sanctuary, which was completed in 1955.

A preliminary architectural rendering of the old First Baptist Church of Greenville, as depicted on an old postcard. When the building was constructed, the original plan was reversed (so the tower would face Main Street), and the detailing was somewhat simplified.

NEW METHODIST CHURCH, PLEASANT RIDGE, OHIO.

Pleasant Ridge Methodist Church, near Cincinnati, Ohio.

First Baptist Church

Greenwood, Leflore County (1907–10)

The old sanctuary of First Baptist Church in Greenwood was one of Mississippi's earliest and finest examples of the Beaux Arts mode of Neoclassical Revival religious architecture. Begun in 1907 and dedicated in 1910, it was located at 500 West Washington Street, at the northwest corner of Washington and Henderson streets.

The designer of the building was C. W. Bulger of Dallas, Texas, who had a large regional practice specializing in church architecture. The building was almost identical in appearance to the former Gaston Avenue Baptist Church (now part of Criswell College) in Dallas, Texas (1902), Beech Street Baptist Church in Texarkana, Arkansas (circa 1909), and the old First Baptist Church of Shreveport, Louisiana (1907) (not extant), which are documented to have been designed by Bulger. Other churches with the same design were the old First Baptist Church in Chickasha, Oklahoma (not extant), and the old St. Luke's

Methodist Church in Oklahoma City (not extant). The old First Baptist Church in Galveston, Texas (1904) (not extant), had a similar design, but it had a recessed main portico instead of a projecting portico.

In the early 1980s a new sanctuary was built for First Baptist Church in Greenwood. The old sanctuary was demolished in 1985.

The old First Baptist Church, Shreveport, Louisiana.

The old St. Luke's Methodist Church, Oklahoma City, Oklahoma.

The old First Baptist Church, Chickasha, Oklahoma.

Beech Street Baptist Church, Texarkana, Arkansas.

Neoclassical Churches in Mississippi, 1905–1927

Nearly all of the architecturally stylish churches built in Mississippi between the late 1870s and about 1905 were designed in a Neo-medieval style—either Gothic or Romanesque Revival, or a combination of the two. The Classical tradition had gone completely out of fashion for religious architecture during that period. Around 1905, however, the Classical tradition began to return to Mississippi's religious architecture, and during the 1910s and 1920s numerous architecturally notable churches were built throughout the state in the Neoclassical style. (The Gothic Revival and Romanesque Revival styles never actually fell out of fashion for religious buildings during this period, however, but continued alongside the Neoclassical Revival.)

The first religious building in Mississippi designed in the new Classical Revival style was apparently Temple B'nai Israel, the Jewish synagogue in Natchez, begun in 1904 and completed in 1905. An almost identical building, Hebrew Union Temple in Greenville, was built in 1906. The same year saw the completion of Temple Beth Israel in Meridian (see page 139). The first Christian house of worship built in the new Classical Revival style was probably the First Baptist Church in Greenwood, which was begun in 1907 and dedicated in 1910 (see page 72).

During the 1910s and 1920s many elegant, dignified Neoclassical Revival churches were built throughout Mississippi, mostly for Baptist, Methodist, and Presbyterian congregations. These churches were nearly all auditorium-plan buildings. Among the more notable surviving examples are Como United Methodist Church (1912), First United Methodist Church in Gulfport (1912–13), First Presbyterian Church in Winona (1913), Galloway Memorial United Methodist Church in Jackson (1913–15), First United Methodist Church in Brookhaven (1916–17), First United Methodist Church in Cleveland (1917), First Baptist Church in Canton (1918), Clarksdale Baptist Church (1919–20), First United Methodist Church in Canton (1922), First Baptist Church in Leland (1922–23), the old sanctuary of First Baptist Church in Clinton (1923), First Baptist Church in Holly Springs (1923), First Baptist Church in New Albany (1923–25), First Presbyterian Church in Starkville (1924–26), First United Methodist Church in Starkville (1925), First Baptist Church in Hazlehurst (1926), and First United Methodist Church in Belzoni (1927).

Notable lost examples include First Baptist Church in Columbia (1911–12), First Methodist Church in Laurel (1912–13), First Methodist Church in Amory (1914), First Baptist Church in Louisville (1915), First Baptist Church in Amory (1916–18), Crystal Springs Methodist Church (1919), Drew Baptist Church (1920), First Baptist Church in Belzoni (1922), First Christian Church in Clarksdale (1923), First Baptist Church in McComb (1923–24), First Baptist Church in Biloxi (1924), and First Baptist Church in Philadelphia (1926).

Neoclassical Revival religious architecture declined in popularity in the late 1920s and very few examples were built after about 1927.

Adapted from "Religious Architecture in Mississippi from the 1820s through the 1920s" in *Historic Churches of Mississippi*.

First Baptist Church

Grenada, Grenada County (1888–91)

The third sanctuary of First Baptist Church of Grenada was begun in 1888, and the first service was held in 1891.[49] Located at the northwest corner of Main Street and Second Street, it was a Gothic auditorium-plan church of brick construction, with a square tower on the north side topped by a tall, slender four-sided spire.

The old Baptist Church of Grenada was very similar to the old First Baptist Church of Ithaca, Michigan (1886) (not extant), which was designed by John Rochester Thomas (1848–1901), of New York, who probably also designed the church in Grenada. The First Baptist Church of Geneseo, New York (not extant), was also quite similar. A surviving building that is nearly identical to these is the Granville Baptist Church in Granville, New York.

By 1925 First Baptist Church of Grenada had been enlarged by an education wing on the north side.[50]

The building burned in 1939.[51] In 1940–41 the present First Baptist Church was built several blocks to the south.

The old First Baptist Church at Ithaca, Michigan.

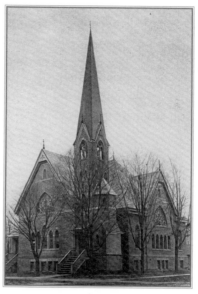

The old First Baptist Church, Geneseo, New York.

First Baptist Church, Grenada, in 1930s, after an education wing had been added to the north side.

St. Mark's Episcopal Church

Mississippi City (later part of Gulfport), Harrison County (1855)

St. Mark's Episcopal Church was organized as a mission in 1846, in Mississippi City, which later became a part of Gulfport.

The building was erected in 1855. It was located on the east side of Church Street, between Sixteenth Street and what is now Beach Boulevard. The church is thought to have originally faced toward the beach, but it was later turned to face northward toward Sixteenth Street. In its original form, it was a traditional simple vernacular church of wood construction, rectangular in plan, with twin front doors on the gabled front façade. It had a simple Greek Revival entablature, and the front gable was detailed as a classical pediment. The interior was remodeled in 1930 and again in 1961. By the 1960s, a belfry had been added, windows had been installed where the twin front doors had been located, and a new entrance had been positioned in the center of the façade.

On August 17, 1969, Hurricane Camille struck the Mississippi Gulf Coast. The storm gutted the building, knocked it from its foundations, and tore off the sacristy at the south end. The adjacent parish hall, Sunday school rooms, and office were destroyed. These facilities were replaced by 1971 and the sanctuary was restored. In 1983 transept wings were added at the back, giving the building a T shape. By that time the entrance had been enclosed within a projecting vestibule.

St. Mark's had been strong enough to endure Hurricane Camille, but it was unable to withstand Hurricane Katrina, which completely destroyed the building when it devastated the Gulf Coast on August 29, 2005.

Since Hurricane Katrina, St. Mark's has moved to a new complex on Taylor Road just west of Lorraine Road, north of Bernard Bayou.

St. Mark's Episcopal Church, as it appeared in 1986. By that time, the twin entrances had been replaced by a center entrance enclosed by a projecting vestibule, and an addition had been built across the back. The classical entablature and the triangular pediment are recognizable from the older picture. The front windows occupied the positions of the original doors.

First Baptist Church

Gulfport, Harrison County (1915)

The second building of First Baptist Church of Gulfport was constructed in 1915 at the southeast corner of Twenty-second Avenue and Fourteenth Street. It was a Neoclassical brick building with two front façades, each with a semi-recessed tetrastyle portico in the Roman Ionic order. Although the building was located on a street corner, the porticoes did not face both intersecting streets. One portico faced westward toward Twenty-second Avenue, but the other faced southward toward Beach Boulevard. Along Fourteenth Street on the north was a rear wall of windows. The exterior wall was curved at the northeast corner, suggesting that the church had a quarter-round auditorium plan with concentric curved seating arranged on a diagonal axis. Surmounting the building was a dome, set upon a cylindrical base (called a drum) that was ringed with round windows. Atop the dome was a small cupola.

An education annex was built to the east of the sanctuary in 1949.

The 1915 sanctuary burned in 1968. It was superseded by a new sanctuary that was built in 1968 just to the south, facing westward onto 22nd Avenue. The 1968 sanctuary survived Hurricane Camille in 1969, but the storm surge of Hurricane

The First Baptist Church, Gulfport, Mississippi

First Baptist Church, Gulfport, viewed from the northwest about 1949–50.

Katrina on August 29, 2005, gutted the building, which was consequently de-molished not long afterwards.

First Baptist Church of Gulfport has moved to a new location, on Highway 605 north of Interstate 10.

St. John the Evangelist Catholic Church

Gulfport, Harrison County (1922–24)

The Spanish Colonial Revival, inspired by the historic Spanish mission churches of California and Texas, became a widely popular architectural style throughout much of the country in the 1920s. It was particularly popular in California, Texas, and Florida, but it was also widely adopted in Alabama, Mississippi, and Louisiana, especially in communities along the Gulf Coast. It served as a romanticized tribute to the Spanish colonial heritage of those areas, but it also inspired thoughts of travel to popular tourist destinations—not just Florida and California, but also Mexico and the Caribbean. In Mississippi, the Spanish Colonial style and the closely related Mission style were widely used for hotels, hospitals, schools, and private homes. There were several Spanish Colonial–style churches built in Mississippi during the 1920s and 1930s, the largest and finest of which was St. John the Evangelist Catholic Church in Gulfport.

Begun in 1922 and completed in 1924, the old St. John's was designed by the architectural firm of Shaw and Wobelen of Gulfport, with John T. Comes of Pittsburgh, Pennsylvania, a noted designer of Catholic churches, as consulting architect. Located on the northeast corner of Twenty-fifth Avenue (U.S. Highway 49) and Seventeenth Street, the church was a large, impressive, twin-towered building, with the stuccoed walls and red tile roofs typical of the Spanish Colonial Revival style.

The old St. John's was seriously damaged by Hurricane Camille on August 17, 1969, and was subsequently demolished. It was replaced in 1971 by the present building of St. John the Evangelist Catholic Church, which was built on the same site.

Main Street Presbyterian Church
(First Presbyterian Church [I])

Hattiesburg, Forrest County (1887, 1900)

Main Street Presbyterian Church was the original building of First Presbyterian Church of Hattiesburg. Built about 1887 and remodeled in 1900,[52] it stood at the northeast corner of Main Street and Jackson Street, on the site later occupied by the old Hattiesburg Public Library, which was built in 1930. This building was superseded by the old First Presbyterian Church (now True Light Missionary Baptist Church), which was built across the street at 836 Main Street in 1929–30.

Old Sacred Heart Catholic Church, Hattiesburg.

Sacred Heart Catholic Church (II)

Hattiesburg, Forrest County (1900)

The first building of Sacred Heart Catholic Church in Hattiesburg was constructed in 1890 at the northeast corner of Walnut Street and Southern Avenue. It burned on March 12, 1900, and a second church was built soon afterward at the same location.[53] The second church was a wood-frame Gothic Revival building with a projecting center front tower. In 1927 the third and present building of Sacred Heart Catholic Church, a substantial brick building, was constructed across the street on the northwest corner of Walnut Street and Southern Avenue,[54] but the old church building remained standing on its original site for another twenty-four years, being used for activities such as Boy Scout meetings. It was torn down in 1951.[55]

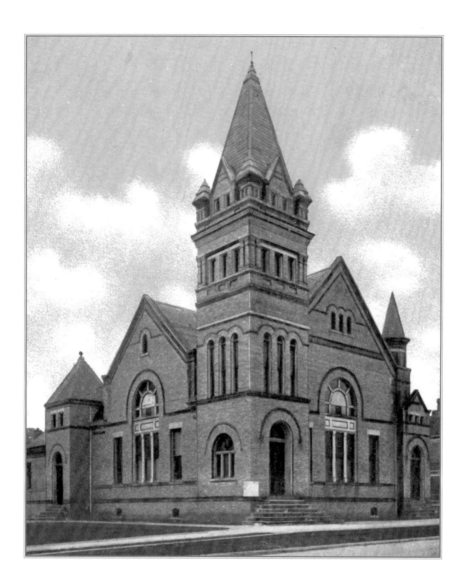

First Baptist Church

Hattiesburg, Forrest County (circa 1901)

The old First Baptist Church of Hattiesburg was a substantial auditorium-plan church in the Romanesque Revival style that was located at the south corner of Buschman Street and South Main Street, facing northwest.[56] It was dedicated on the third Sunday of April 1901.[57] Although the architect of the building has not been documented, the building was very similar to several buildings that are known to have been designed by R. H. Hunt,[58] particularly Moore Memorial Methodist Church in Winona, Mississippi (1898),[59] the old sanctuary of First

Baptist Church of Elberton, Georgia (1897), and Central Methodist Church (not extant) in Albany, now part of Decatur, Alabama (circa 1898).

The old First Baptist Church in Hattiesburg was remodeled in 1915,[60] and an education building was built southwest of the main building about 1939. In 1953 the congregation moved to a new building at 501 West Pine Street,[61] and the old church complex was later demolished. A park now occupies the site.

The old First Baptist Church, Hattiesburg, viewed from the west.

The old sanctuary of First Baptist Church, Elberton, Georgia.

The old Central Methodist Church in Albany (later part of Decatur), Alabama.

Hazlehurst Baptist Church (II)

Hazlehurst, Copiah County (1892–93)

The second building of Hazlehurst Baptist Church stood at the southeast corner of East Gallatin (Estelle) Street and East Railroad Avenue. Built in 1892–93, it was designed by R. H. Hunt, of Chattanooga, Tennessee.[62] This building was the Baptist church of Hazlehurst until 1926, when the congregation moved to the present building on South Extension Street,[63] which was also designed by R. H. Hunt. The old Baptist Church later served for a time as the Hazlehurst public library.[64]

First Baptist Church

Iuka, Tishomingo County (1915)

The old First Baptist Church in Iuka, built in 1915, was one of three almost identical examples of the smaller version of the quarter-round Neoclassical churches designed by James E. Greene.[65] Unlike the more widespread larger version, which was two stories tall, the smaller version was only one story in height, and had an unusual three-column semi-recessed portico on both of its two façades. Besides this building, the other two identified examples are the old First Baptist Church in Ripley (1916) (not extant) (see page 169) and Chalybeate Baptist Church in Tippah County (1918), which still stands.

This building stood at the southeast corner of Eastport and Tate streets in Iuka. The present (fourth) sanctuary of First Baptist Church now occupies the site.

The original Methodist Church in Jackson as it appeared in a photograph made by Elisaeus von Seutter in the 1870s.

Christ Church, Tuscaloosa, Alabama, as it appeared before being extensively remodeled in 1880.

Methodist Church
(Methodist Episcopal Church) (I)

Jackson, Hinds County (1838–39)

The original building of what would later become the First Methodist Episcopal Church of Jackson, and eventually Galloway Memorial United Methodist Church, was built in 1838–39.[66] It stood at the site currently occupied by Galloway's sanctuary, at the northwest corner of North Congress Street and Yazoo Street, but it faced southward, toward Smith Park, instead of toward Congress Street. It was a rectangular, gable-roofed church of brick construction. As depicted in early photographs, the brick walls appear to have been stuccoed. The building had twin round-arched doors on the front gable end and round-arched windows on the side walls. It shared certain details with the original design of Christ Episcopal Church in Tuscaloosa, Alabama (1829–30),[67] which was designed by the noted English-born architect William Nichols. Nichols, who was in Jackson at the time supervising the construction of the Old State Capitol, designed the original Presbyterian Church building in Jackson (see page 94) and was evidently the architect of this church as well.

The old Methodist Church building survived the Civil War, but it was demolished about 1882 to allow for the construction of the second building of what was then called First Methodist Episcopal Church, South, which was built in 1882–83 (see page 105).

First Presbyterian Church (I)

Jackson, Hinds County (1843–46)

The original building of First Presbyterian Church of Jackson was designed by William Nichols, the architect of the Old Capitol. A rectangular brick building with a pedimented front gable and topped by a cylindrical belfry, it was somewhat similar in appearance to the Methodist Church that was built nearby in 1838–39. The cornerstone of the Presbyterian Church was laid on October 10, 1843, and the building was opened for services on February 1, 1846.[68] It was located at the northwest corner of State Street and Yazoo Street.

Like the antebellum Methodist Church, the Presbyterian Church survived the Civil War, but it was demolished in the late nineteenth century. The last service was held in this building on July 19, 1891.[69] It was demolished soon thereafter to allow for the construction of the second building of First Presbyterian Church, which was built on the same site in 1892 (see page 108).

Farewell View of the Old Presbyterian Church,
JACKSON, MISS.,
TAKEN ON MONDAY AFTERNOON, JULY 20, 1891.

A "farewell view" photograph of the original First Presbyterian Church in Jackson, made shortly before its demolition in 1891.

First Christian Church (I)

Jackson, Hinds County (circa 1845–50)

The first building erected for the Disciples of Christ (Christian) congregation in Jackson stood at the northeast corner of Mississippi Street and President Street, where the Chapel of First Baptist Church is now located. It was a rectangular, gable-roofed brick church with a central front door on the gable end, facing southward toward Mississippi Street. Atop the roof ridge was a small, square belfry trimmed with corner pilasters and topped by a shallow pyramidal cap surmounted by a pinnacle. The date of construction is not recorded, but the church was evidently erected sometime around 1845–50. "All that is known is that it was constructed before the Civil War and was a substantial brick building . . ."[70]

The church survived the Civil War, but by the 1880s the building was in very poor structural condition. The first Sanborn insurance map of Jackson, dated September 1885, shows the building with the notation "uninsurable on account of badly cracked walls." It was demolished soon afterwards, probably later in 1885.[71] The May 1890 Sanborn map shows that it had been removed from the site by that time, and a small wood-frame chapel had been erected on the north end of the lot, facing toward President Street. The wooden building was apparently intended to serve only temporarily. A larger brick church was built in 1893 on the site of the first building (see page 110).

St. Peter's Catholic Church (II)

Jackson, Hinds County (1867–69)

The original building of St. Peter's Catholic Church in Jackson was a small wood-frame structure erected in 1846 at the northwest corner of President and Court streets. That building was burned by Union troops during the Civil War, when forces under the command of General William T. Sherman occupied the city May 14–16, 1863, causing widespread destruction.[72]

In 1867 a new church, also of wood-frame construction, was built at what is now the southwest corner of West and Amite streets, where the rectory of St. Peter's is now located. (Amite Street did not extend westward beyond West Street at that time.) The second church was dedicated in 1869.

After the third St. Peter's Church (now St. Peter's Cathedral) was built in 1900, the old wooden church building was reduced in size (with the cupola,

The former building of St. Peter's Catholic Church, after it was moved about 1913 and remodeled to become Holy Ghost Catholic Church. Notice that the cupola and the transepts had been removed, and a new bell tower had been added at the rear of the building.

transepts, and chancel having been removed) and was used on its original site for several years as a Knights of Columbus hall. About 1913, the building was moved approximately one mile north to what was then called Short Blair Street (later renamed Cloister Street), where it became the place of worship for Holy Ghost Catholic Church, an African American congregation. In 1970 a new Holy Ghost Church was built across the street at 1151 Cloister Street. The old church was later demolished.

St. Andrew's Episcopal Church (II)

Jackson, Hinds County (1869–73)

The original building of St Andrew's Episcopal Church in Jackson stood on Capitol Street, at about the location of the Lamar Life Building. It was begun in 1846, completed in 1849, and consecrated in 1850.[73] As early as 1860, however, plans were being made to replace it with a new building, but those plans were disrupted by the Civil War.

On June 1, 1869, the cornerstone was laid for the second building of St. Andrew's.[74] The building was sufficiently complete to be occupied in November 1870, but was not finished until 1873.[75] It was built by P. McHenry Boliner, from plans drawn up by an architect named Stuart.[76] Located at the southeast corner of Capitol Street and Congress Street, it was a rectangular brick building in the Romanesque Revival style, with round-arched openings and a slightly projecting tower at the center of the façade. The tower did not have a spire, although one was undoubtedly originally intended. The April 10, 1873, issue of the *Weekly Clarion* reported the completion of the building and contained a detailed description.[77]

The present St. Andrew's Episcopal Cathedral, located one block to the west on Capitol Street, was completed in 1903,[78] and the second building was demolished in late 1904 or early 1905. Some of the windows and furnishings from the second building were moved into the chapel of the later St. Andrew's Cathedral. In 1905 the Jones-Kennington Dry Goods Company building (also known as Kennington's Department Store, later McRae's Department Store, and more recently the Heritage Building) was built on the site of the second building.

Temple Beth Israel (II)

Jackson, Hinds County (1874–75)

Congregation Beth Israel ("House of Israel") in Jackson was organized in 1860. In 1867 the congregation erected a wooden synagogue at the southeast corner of South State Street and South Street. The original building, the first Jewish house of worship in Mississippi, was destroyed by a fire on July 10, 1874.[79]

The second building of Temple Beth Israel was constructed on the same site in 1874–75 and was dedicated on June 25, 1875.[80] The architect of the building was Joseph Willis. He also designed the old Rankin County Courthouse in Brandon (1853) and the Madison County Courthouse in Canton (1854–57), and he directed the remodeling of the Old State Capitol in 1870–71.

The second temple was a two-story brick building with Gothic style pointed-arch windows. Although the Gothic Revival was promoted by some architectural theorists of the mid-nineteenth century as being a distinctly Christian style, it was also used for the design of some Jewish synagogues in the later years of the

Temple Beth Israel in Jackson in the late 1930s. Notice that the pair of curving stairs shown in the 1870s photograph had been replaced by a single straight stair and that the walls had been stuccoed.

nineteenth century. (Temple Anshe Chesed in Vicksburg, built in 1868–70, was originally very similar in appearance, but it was later altered by the addition of a new Romanesque façade in 1893.)[81]

As originally constructed, the second Temple Beth Israel had a pair of curving staircases leading to the auditorium on the upper story, but these were later removed and replaced by a single, straight staircase that was slightly wider at the foot than at the top. The building was originally finished in exposed brick, but the walls were later stuccoed.

By the 1930s, the area along South State Street where the synagogue was located, which had been a residential neighborhood in the late nineteenth century, was becoming increasingly industrial. In 1940 the congregation relocated to a new synagogue on Woodrow Wilson Boulevard (see page 118) and the second Temple Beth Israel, which had served as a synagogue for sixty-five years, was demolished. The site of the first and second synagogues was shown on the Sanborn fire insurance map of Jackson in 1946 as a vacant lot. A gas station now occupies that location. A state historical marker commemorating the first and second synagogues was placed at the site in 2005.

Jewish Synagogues in Mississippi

In the decade prior to the Civil War, the Jewish population of Mississippi was growing substantially, and several communities had populations large enough to organize congregations for worship, but no synagogue buildings were built in Mississippi until after the war.

In the ten years immediately following the end of the Civil War, at least five synagogues were constructed in Mississippi, and several more were built between 1875 and 1900. The first synagogue built in the state was the original building of Beth Israel in Jackson. It was a wood-frame building erected in 1867 on the southeast corner of State Street and South Street. It burned in 1874 and was replaced later that year by a brick building at the same location (see page 101). Other nineteenth-century synagogues were built in Vicksburg (1868–70, enlarged in 1893), Summit (circa 1870), Natchez (1870–72), Meridian (circa 1875) (see page 139), Canton (1877) (see page 34), Port Gibson (1891–92), Brookhaven (1896), and Woodville (1896). Of these, only the buildings at Port Gibson and Brookhaven still stand.

Several synagogues were built in the very early years of the twentieth century, including those at Natchez (1904–5), Lexington (1905), Meridian (1906) (not extant), and Greenville (1906). Greenwood had two early twentieth-century synagogues, Beth Israel (1918) (not extant) and Ahavath Rayim (1923). Others were built in Cleveland, Clarksdale, and several other communities. After World War II the Jewish population in Mississippi shifted primarily to the larger cities, while congregations in the smaller towns declined. Only a few of these older synagogues still stand, and even fewer are still in active use.

For further information about Mississippi's historic Jewish congregations, contact the Goldring/ Woldenberg Institute of Southern Jewish Life, in Jackson, or visit their Web site at www.isjl.org.

The second building of First Methodist Episcopal Church, Jackson, photographed by Albert F. Daniel in 1907.

First Methodist Church
(First Methodist Episcopal Church, South) (II)

Jackson, Hinds County (1883)

The second building of what was then called First Methodist Episcopal Church in Jackson was built in 1883, on the site of the earlier church, at the northwest corner of North Congress Street and Yazoo Street, though it faced eastward toward Congress Street instead of southward toward Smith Park as the original church had done. The architect and builder was H. M. Taylor, who also built the First Christian Church in 1893 (see page 110).

This building was demolished about 1913 to allow for the construction of the present sanctuary of Galloway Memorial United Methodist Church on the same site.[82]

St. Columb's Chapel

Jackson, Hinds County (1892)

Completed about 1892, St. Columb's Chapel in Jackson was located adjacent to Battle Hill, the residence of the bishop of the Episcopal Diocese of Mississippi.[83] The house was located at 1200 West Capitol Street, and the chapel was built a short distance to the east, just north of what is now the intersection of West Monument Street and Bratton Street.[84]

Built of native stone that had been previously used for the old Hinds County jail at Raymond,[85] the chapel was a "low Gothic" building that had narrow lancet windows in the chancel (at the southeast end), and broad, low, tripartite Tudor-arched windows illuminating the nave. It was entered from a low porch at the center of the southwest side, above which was a short, rectangular bell tower without a spire. The chapel eventually served as the model for Grace Episcopal Church in Okolona, built in 1907–8, and Church of the Resurrection in Starkville, built in 1913.[86]

St. Columb's was built at the behest of Bishop Hugh Miller Thompson as a memorial to his predecessor, Bishop William Mercer Green. Bishop Thompson intended for the chapel to become the chancel of a much larger church, which would have served as the cathedral of the Diocese of Mississippi. The chapel was consecrated on April 26, 1894, as St. Columb's Cathedral, and it served as the cathedral of the diocese until Bishop Thompson's death in 1902.[87]

After Bishop Thompson's death, interest in St. Columb's diminished. This was perhaps due in part to the completion, in 1903, of a large and substantial new building for St. Andrew's Episcopal Church in downtown Jackson, scarcely a mile away.[88] The congregation of St. Columb's disbanded in 1905 and the chapel later burned.[89] By November 1946, the city bus garage had been built on the northeastern part of the site where the chapel had stood.[90] In 1950–51 the site of Battle Hill and the remainder of the site of St. Columb's Chapel were leased for commercial development[91] and became part of the Battle Hill Village Shopping Center, which was built in 1952.[92] (It was later renamed Mid-City Mart Shopping Center, and is now West Park Mart Shopping Center).

The name "St. Columb's" was later revived for a new Episcopal congregation in west Jackson that was organized as a mission in 1941 and became a parish in 1948.[93] Formerly located at 301 Claiborne Avenue in Jackson, the church moved to 550 Sunnybrook Road in Ridgeland in 1998.[94]

First Presbyterian Church (II)

Jackson, Hinds County (1892–93)

In 1891, the old Presbyterian Church that had stood at the northwest corner of State Street and Yazoo Street in Jackson since 1846 was demolished, and construction began on a new building on the same site. Dedicated on May 14, 1893,[95] this new building was a Gothic Revival auditorium-plan church of brick construction.

The architect for the new church was Reuben Harrison Hunt (1862–1937), a regionally prominent architect of Chattanooga, Tennessee, who designed many notable churches, schools, and government buildings throughout the

The old First Presbyterian Church, Jackson, being demolished in 1951.

South from the 1880s through the 1920s.[96] Among the other churches Hunt designed in Mississippi were the old Hazlehurst Baptist Church (1892), the old First Baptist Church in Meridian (1892–93), the First United Methodist Church in Greenwood (1898), and the Moore Memorial United Methodist Church in Winona (1898).[97]

The contractor for First Presbyterian Church was J. F. Barnes, of Greenville, Mississippi,[98] who built the old Bolivar County Courthouse in Rosedale (1889) (not extant) and the present Washington County Courthouse in Greenville (1891). About the same time that the First Presbyterian Church was under construction, Barnes was also building the Jewish synagogue in Port Gibson, Temple Gemiluth Chassed (1891–92).[99]

In 1951 the congregation of First Presbyterian Church moved to a new complex about a mile to the north at 1390 North State Street. The final service in the old church was on August 29, 1951.[100] The building was demolished later that year. The former Jackson Municipal Library was built on the site in 1954.[101] A state historical marker in front of the old library building indicates the site of the old First Presbyterian Church. The date stone of the 1892 church building has been set into the front wall of the present sanctuary.

First Christian Church (III)

Jackson, Hinds County (1893)

The third building[102] of First Christian Church in Jackson was constructed in 1893 at the northeast corner of North President Street and Mississippi Street, at the same site where the original building had been located. It was built by H. M. Taylor, a prominent building contractor and civic leader who also built the First Methodist Church in 1883 and did much of the construction of the second building of First Baptist Church between 1891 and 1900.[103] Taylor used a picture of the First Christian Church of Jackson in an advertisement for his firm that ran in 1894 in several issues of *The Messenger*, a weekly newspaper published for the Christian (Disciples of Christ) denomination in Mississippi.

When the church was built, it was located across President Street from the state penitentiary, but the New Capitol was later constructed on the site of the prison, and after its completion in 1903 the church achieved a new prominence by being located directly across the street from the state capitol.

The building, as originally built, was a nearly square Romanesque Revival auditorium-plan church of brick construction, with a three-stage pyramidal-roofed tower at the southwest corner. The main roof of the building was also pyramidal, but it had lower cross-gables on all four sides. In the gable walls of the prominent south and west façades were large circular stained-glass windows. The window on the south wall was adorned with a pattern of circles, and the one on the west had a tracery pattern in the form of a six-pointed star (Star of David).[104] About 1912 the building was enlarged by the addition of flat-roofed wings on all four sides,[105] which somewhat obscured the original Romanesque Revival styling and gave the church a touch of Prairie Style character.

On July 1, 1950, the congregation relocated to a new building at the northeast corner of State Street and High Street.[106] The old building was demolished not long afterwards, and the chapel of First Baptist Church was later built on the site.

An advertisement for H. M. Taylor, Contractor and Builder, that appeared in the February 1, 1894, issue of The Messenger, a weekly newspaper published for the Disciples of Christ in Mississippi.

First Christian Church as it appeared in the 1930s, with the flat-roofed wings that were added about 1912.

First Baptist Church (II)

Jackson, Hinds County (1891–1900)

The original building of First Baptist Church in Jackson was a Greek Revival structure, erected in 1843–44, that still stands at the northeast corner of Mississippi and West streets, facing Smith Park.[107] When that building became too small, a new church was built at the northwest corner of Capitol Street and President Street.

The second building was begun in 1891. The first service was held there in November 1894, but the main auditorium was not available for use until April 9, 1899.[108] Some work, however, remained to be done as late as 1900, for the building is shown on the Sanborn insurance map of May 1900 with the notation "not completed." The indebtedness was paid off on February 1, 1901, and the building was dedicated on March 10, 1901.[109]

The building was a large Romanesque Revival style auditorium-plan church with concentric curved seating "in a semi-circular pattern." [110] The Capitol Street façade was dominated by a tall tower topped by a slender spire. The church was designed by Lawrence B. Valk and Company of New York. (Valk was also the architect of the First Baptist Church in Colorado Springs, Colorado, which, although the design of the tower is different, bears a strong resemblance to the old First Baptist Church of Jackson.) The original contractor for the First Baptist Church in Jackson was H. M. Taylor, who later completed the building; but records indicate that some of the construction work was done by J. M. Barnes of Greenville, Mississippi. [111] In 1927 the congregation of First Baptist Church of Jackson moved to their present location at the corner of North President Street and College Street, across President Street from the New Capitol. The last service was held in the old building on May 30, 1926. [112] It was demolished later in 1926, and the property was sold for commercial development in January 1927. [113] Several small commercial buildings were later built on the site, including the building on the corner that was long occupied by a Krystal restaurant.

First Baptist Church, Colorado Springs, Colorado.

The old Griffith Memorial Baptist Church, Jackson.

Griffith Memorial Baptist Church

Jackson, Hinds County (1907)

Griffith Memorial Baptist Church was built in 1907[114] at the southeast corner of Winter and Hunter streets, next to the original building of J. Z. George School. It was a wooden auditorium-plan church with round-arched windows and a corner tower embellished with classical corner pilasters and classical pediments supporting a pyramidal spire. It was superseded by the present building of Griffith Memorial which was constructed nearby in 1930.[115]

First Church of Christ, Scientist

Jackson, Hinds County (1911)

The old First Church of Christ, Scientist, in Jackson occupied the northeast corner of North State Street and Fortification Street from 1911 until about 1959. Designed by Robert C. Spencer, of Chicago, it was a Tudor style church with faux half-timbered walls. The former Jitney Jungle No. 14 grocery store, built two blocks to the east in 1929, has similar detailing.

The congregation relocated to a new building at 755 Riverside Drive about 1959. This former church building had begun to be used as a commercial building by 1960, when it is listed in the city directory as the location of Odom's Optical. Odom's occupied the building for over thirty years before relocating to Canton Mart Road. The old church burned on January 31, 1995, while being demolished. The site is now occupied by a McDonald's restaurant.

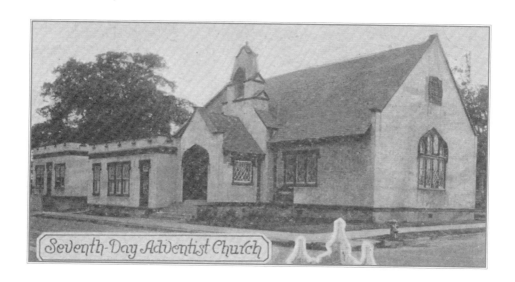

Seventh-Day Adventist Church

Seventh Day Adventist Church

Jackson, Hinds County (circa 1915)

South Gallatin Street in Jackson is now a light industrial area, but in the first two or three decades of the twentieth century, the area was largely residential. That is what led the Seventh Day Adventists to build a church at 701 South Gallatin Street (at the southwest corner of Gallatin and Hooker streets) about 1915.[116] The structure was built by the prominent Jackson contractor I. C. Garber, who also built Capitol Street Methodist Church (1910–12), Galloway Memorial Methodist Church (1913–15), First Baptist Church of Jackson (1924–27), and other notable churches in Jackson and other communities.[117] The Seventh Day Adventist Church was a stucco-clad brick building with residential-scale proportions and an informal "low Gothic" architectural character.

About 1965 the congregation relocated, and soon thereafter the former church building became the first home of New Stage Theatre. New Stage moved to their present location at 1100 Carlisle Street in Belhaven in 1978,[118] and the former church was later demolished.

Temple Beth Israel (III)

Jackson, Hinds County (1940)

In 1940, Congregation Beth Israel of Jackson relocated from its small nineteenth-century synagogue on South State Street to a new building at 546 East Woodrow Wilson Boulevard, just west of State Street, next door to the Mississippi Federation of Women's Clubs building.

The congregation did not stay at that location for very long, however, for in 1967, just twenty-seven years later, they moved to their present location at 5315 Old Canton Road.[119] The building on Woodrow Wilson Boulevard was apparently demolished not long afterwards. The site is now occupied by offices of the Mississippi Department of Health.

PRESBYTERIAN CHURCH LAUREL, MISS.

First Presbyterian Church

Laurel, Jones County (1901–2)

A particularly interesting and elaborate example of a wooden church with Shingle Style features was the old First Presbyterian Church of Laurel. It stood at the northwest corner of Fifth Avenue and Fifth Street, where the present building of First-Trinity Presbyterian Church now stands. This church was originally built in 1901, but was destroyed by a fire on December 10, 1901.[120] As rebuilt in 1902, it was reported to have been identical to the original building except that it was ten feet longer.[121] The upper half of its distinctive octagonal bell tower was clad in shingle siding.

It was demolished about 1924, to allow for the construction of the present sanctuary on the same site.[122]

First Methodist Church

Laurel, Jones County (1912–13)

The old First Methodist Church in Laurel (originally Main Street Methodist Episcopal Church, South) was built in 1912–13. It was located on the west side of Fifth Avenue (originally called Main Street), between Yates Avenue and Fifth Street, directly across Fifth Avenue from the Jones County Courthouse.

This building was demolished about 1957 and was replaced on the same site by the present sanctuary of First United Methodist Church.

First Baptist Church

Laurel, Jones County (1920)

The auditorium-plan church, a design characterized by a wide preaching hall with theater-style concentric curved seating, was introduced into Mississippi around 1885 and became very widespread by the mid-1890s. It continued to be popular for the design of churches well into the 1920s. Most auditorium-plan churches built in Mississippi before about 1910 were Neo-medieval in style—either Gothic or Romanesque—but by the later 1910s auditorium-plan churches were more commonly being built in the Neoclassical style. Although some notable examples of Gothic and Romanesque Revival auditorium-plan churches continued to be built into the early 1920s, it became more common by the 1920s for Gothic Revival churches to have a more traditional axial plan with a prominent center aisle.

One of the most impressive of the later examples of a Gothic Revival auditorium-plan church was erected in 1920 for the First Baptist Church in Laurel. It stood at the northwest corner of Fifth Street and Sixth Avenue, facing southward toward Fifth Street.

It was demolished about 1960, to allow for the construction of the present sanctuary of First Baptist Church, which was built on the same site in 1961.

All Saints Episcopal Church, Long Beach, as pictured on an early postcard.

All Saints Episcopal Church

Long Beach, Harrison County (1895)

All Saints Episcopal Church in Long Beach was a Carpenter Gothic church built in 1895.

In 1920 the congregation of All Saints disbanded. The building was demolished sometime thereafter, and some of its materials were used for the construction of McGinnis-Wharton Hall of First Presbyterian Church in 1936.

Louisville Presbyterian Church

Louisville, Winston County (circa 1890)

For over a century, the town of Louisville has had multiple Presbyterian congregations of different affiliations. From the time of the Civil War until the 1970s, most of Mississippi's Presbyterian congregations were affiliated with the Presbyterian Church in the United States (the PCUS, or "southern" Presbyterians), along with a scattering of Cumberland Presbyterian and Associate Reformed Presbyterian churches. During that period there were also a few congregations affiliated with the Presbyterian Church, USA (the "northern" Presbyterians). One of these rare "northern" congregations was the Louisville Presbyterian Church. A few blocks away, the First Presbyterian Church was a PCUS congregation.[123]

About 1890 a wood-frame building was erected for Louisville Presbyterian Church at the southwest corner of Church Street and College Street. It was apparently built from a mail-order plan prepared by Benjamin D. Price. This plan, which is shown as Perspective No. 19A in the 1906 edition of *Church Plans*, was one of Price's most popular designs during the 1880s and 1890s. More than eighty churches were built throughout the country using this design.

The wooden church was replaced in 1917 by the present sanctuary of Louisville Presbyterian Church.

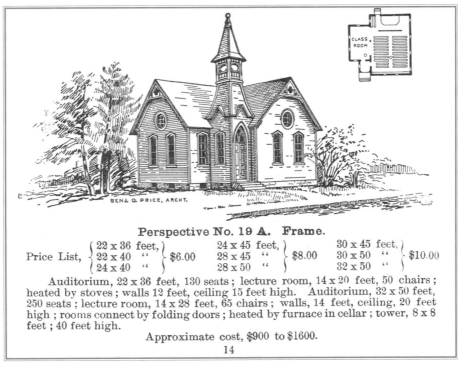

Perspective No. 19A, from *Church Plans* (1906) by Benjamin D. Price and Max Charles Price.

Grace Linn Methodist Church in Hartland, Maine, was another of the many churches throughout the country that were built from the plan depicted in Perspective No. 19A.

First Baptist Church

Louisville, Winston County (1915)

The old First Baptist Church of Louisville, built in 1915, was located at the southeast corner of South Church Avenue and West Park Street. Like several other Mississippi churches of the same design, it was a domed Neoclassical building, built of brick, with two matching front façades, each with a semi-recessed tetrastyle portico in the Roman Ionic order, and a curving rear wall that gave the building a distinctive quarter-round shape. This building was almost identical in appearance to the old First Baptist Church in Columbia (1911–12) (see page 43) and the old First Methodist Church in Amory (1914) (see page 10).

The present sanctuary of First Baptist Church of Louisville was built in 1953 immediately to the south of the old church, which was demolished not long afterwards.

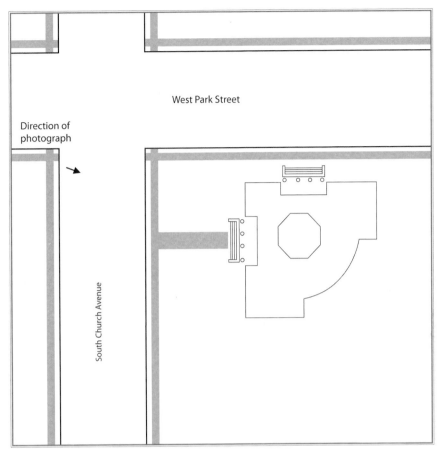

West Park Street

Direction of photograph

South Church Avenue

The site plan of the old First Baptist Church, Louisville, showing the distinctive quarter-round shape.

The old First Baptist Church, Macon.

First Baptist Church (II)

Macon, Noxubee County (1852)

Erected in 1852, the second building of First Baptist Church of Macon was a small Greek Revival church of wood-frame construction, which stood at the northwest corner of Lawrence Street and North Street. According to the *History of the First Baptist Church, 1835–1960*, "an Irishman, by the name of A. M. O'Connelly, who had recently come to Macon from New Orleans, was engaged as architect and builder."[124] The church was a rectangular temple-form building on a raised brick basement. Across the front was a tetrastyle portico in the Tuscan order. The steps to the main entrance were placed behind the columns of the portico. A small, square belfry stood atop the roof ridge.

This building was demolished in 1907 to allow for the construction of the third and present sanctuary of First Baptist Church on the same site.[125]

The old Macon Presbyterian Church, as pictured on a very early twentieth-century postcard.

Macon Presbyterian Church

Macon, Noxubee County (1890)

The old Macon Presbyterian Church was built in 1890 at the southwest corner of Wayne and Eighth streets in Macon. It was largely Victorian Gothic in style, but its eclectic design incorporated a variety of unusual elements that can be seen on certain other religious buildings around Mississippi. The octagonal steeple with a triangular gablet on each face resembles the spire of St. Mary's Episcopal Church in Lexington.[126] On the second story of the tower is an unusual Moorish-style window in the same shape as some of those in the façade of the B'nai Sholom Synagogue in Brookhaven.[127] Several churches of this period had a diagonally canted corner tower, but no other church in the state had a tower jutting out at this odd angle from the side of the building. The roof, too, had an unusual configuration. The architect of this fascinating composition has not been identified.

This building burned in 1941. It was replaced in 1947 by a new sanctuary of Macon Presbyterian Church on the same site.

First Baptist Church (II)

Magnolia, Pike County (1895)

At the beginning of the twentieth century the town of Magnolia had two large, substantial auditorium-plan churches built of wood. The older of the two was the second building of First Baptist Church, which was erected in 1895 on the east side of Clark Avenue between Laurel Street and Bay Street. With pointed arches on the porch and the windows, including several slender lancet windows on the tower, the building was largely Gothic Revival in style, though the square tower capped by a pyramidal roof was a typical feature of Romanesque-inspired buildings.

The church was demolished about 1937 and replaced by a new building at the same location. The third building was, in turn, replaced by the present fourth sanctuary of First Baptist Church, which was built on the same site in 1962–63.

Magnolia Methodist Church
(Methodist Episcopal Church, South)

Magnolia, Pike County (1898)

The second of Magnolia's elaborate wood-frame auditorium-plan churches was built for the Magnolia Methodist Episcopal Church in 1898, at the southeast corner of Clark Avenue and Myrtle Street, across Clark Avenue from the Presbyterian church that was built in 1881–82. The cornerstone of the Methodist church was laid on March 9, 1898, and the first service in the completed church was held on October 16 of that year.[128] The building was distinguished by an unusually ornate tower, and the arches above all of the windows contained complex patterns of tracery. The north end of the building was semioctagonal, with each bay containing a tall window capped by a gablet.

This building was demolished in 1947 and the present third sanctuary of what is now called First United Methodist Church was completed the following year on the same site.

The Catholic Church and Convent,
McComb City, Mississippi.

A2914 PUBLISHED FOR THE MC COMB CITY DRUG STORE,
MC COMB CITY, MISS.

St. Alphonsus Catholic Church

McComb, Pike County (1875–76)

The first building of St. Alphonsus Catholic Church in McComb (formerly called McComb City) was a rectangular wooden church with round-arched windows and a small projecting entrance vestibule. Its most distinctive feature was a steeple with a flared base trimmed with pairs of Italianate brackets at the eaves. Built in 1875–76, the church was located at the southwest corner of Delaware Avenue and Fifth Street. Immediately adjacent to the church were the priest's residence, a convent, and a parochial school.

In 1922, the wooden building was replaced on the same site by the present sanctuary of St. Alphonsus, a twin-towered, brick Italian Romanesque building.[129]

First Baptist Church (III)

McComb, Pike County (1905)

The third building of First Baptist Church of McComb, built in 1905, was a brick Gothic Revival auditorium-plan church that stood at the east corner of Delaware Avenue and Fourth Street.

It was replaced by a Neoclassical building on the same site in 1923–24 (see page 138).

629 B First Methodist Church,
McComb City, Miss.

The second building of Centenary Methodist Church, McComb.

Centenary Methodist Church
(Methodist Episcopal Church, South) (II)

McComb, Pike County (1906)

The oldest Methodist congregation in McComb was organized in the early 1870s, and began construction on their first building in 1884. Like many Methodist churches throughout the United States that either were founded in that year or erected new buildings about that time, they adopted the name Centenary in commemoration of the one-hundredth anniversary of the founding of Methodism as a denomination. Completed in 1885, it was located on a narrow triangular lot at the corner of Broadway and Third Street, facing north toward the major intersection where Broadway, Third Street, Delaware Avenue, and Main Street all converge.

Within two decades, a new building was needed. The second building of Centenary Methodist Church was completed in 1906. It was located on the same site as the first building, immediately next door to where the McComb City Hall would be built in 1914–15. The 1906 building was an auditorium-plan church of brick construction. Its stylistic character was largely Romanesque (as indicated by the round-arched openings), embellished with Gothic-style stepped diagonal buttresses on the front tower.

In 1926, the congregation moved to its present home at 500 Delaware Avenue (across the street from St. Alphonsus Catholic Church), and the old building was demolished soon thereafter.

First Baptist Church (IV)

McComb, Pike County (1923–24)

The fourth building of First Baptist Church in McComb was erected in 1923–24 on the same site as the earlier church (see page 135), on the west corner of Delaware Avenue and Fourth Street. It was a Neoclassical building built of brick, with a very shallow false portico[130] that did not shelter the entrances, which were on either side of the portico. The old First Baptist Church of Biloxi, built in 1924 (see page 21), had the same configuration.

About 1970 First Baptist Church of McComb moved to a new building at 1700 Delaware Avenue. The old church building was demolished about 1971.

Temple Beth Israel (I)

Meridian, Lauderdale County (circa 1875)

The Jewish congregation of Beth Israel in Meridian was organized in 1868. Sometime around 1870 to 1875 the first synagogue was built, located on the small triangular block formed by Hale, Garland, and High Streets (now Twenty-second Avenue, Eighth Street, and Sixth Street). It was a rectangular, gable-roofed building of brick construction with round-arched windows. The entrance, at the center of the front (west) façade, was flanked by short twin towers, each topped by a square ogival dome surmounted by a pinnacle, giving the building a Moorish appearance.

In 1906 the congregation moved to a new building at the corner of Twenty-fourth Avenue and Eleventh Street (see page 147), and the old synagogue was promptly demolished. The Sanborn fire insurance map of Meridian made in August 1906 shows a new commercial building already occupying the site.

The Church of the Mediator in Meridian photographed in the 1870s or early 1880s.

The Church of the Mediator as pictured in the Meridian City Directory of 1888.

Church of the Mediator (Episcopal)

Meridian, Lauderdale County (1876–78)

The Church of the Mediator was organized in 1858 as the first Episcopal congregation in Meridian. Nearly twenty years after the founding of the parish, a wood-frame Carpenter Gothic church building was constructed at the northeast corner of Twenty-fourth Avenue and Ninth Street (at the opposite end of the block on which the present First Presbyterian Church now stands). The cornerstone was laid on March 7, 1876, and the building was finished in 1878.[131] It had an octagonal steeple with a tall spire, and the entrance was flanked by tall stepped buttresses (which, on a wooden building, served no structural purpose and were entirely decorative).

In 1911, the Church of the Mediator merged with St. Paul's Episcopal Church, which had been organized in 1901. The united congregation met at the larger building that had been constructed for St. Paul's in 1902, and retained the name St. Paul's.[132] Sometime after the merger, the former Church of the Mediator building was sold to the Church of Christ, Scientist. The building appears as the Church of Christ, Scientist on the Sanborn fire insurance map of 1950. The Christian Science Church later moved to a new facility at 4009 Jaycee Drive, after which the old church building was demolished.

An Episcopal congregation called the Church of the Mediator was reestablished in 1952 and built a new church building in 1960.[133] Two stained-glass windows that had been salvaged from the old church were installed in the parish hall built in 1988.

First Methodist Church,
Meridian, Miss.

Central Methodist Church (III)
(Methodist Episcopal Church, South)

Meridian, Lauderdale County (1885)

The third building of Central Methodist Church in Meridian was built in 1885.[134] A Victorian Gothic church of brick construction, it stood at the south corner of Twenty-third Avenue (originally Rodes Street) and Eighth Street (originally Garland Street) until it burned in 1913. After the fire, the congregation met at the Lauderdale County Courthouse until the original part of the present Central

United Methodist Church was completed in 1919.[135] The Niolon Building was built on the site of the old church in 1914.

Central Methodist Church as pictured in the Meridian City Directory of 1888.

First Baptist Church

Meridian, Lauderdale County (1892–93)

A large and architecturally notable example of the Romanesque Revival auditorium-plan churches built in Mississippi during the 1890s was the First Baptist Church of Meridian, which was located at the northwest corner of Seventh Street and Twenty-sixth Avenue. Begun in 1892 and completed in 1893, it replaced an earlier Gothic Revival church that had stood on the same site. The architect was R. H. Hunt of Chattanooga, Tennessee.[136]

The 1906 Sanborn insurance map of Meridian shows that an addition had been made to the east end of the building by that time. Later that addition was replaced by a much larger education building, which appears on the 1950 Sanborn map.

In 1959 the building was replaced on the same site by the present sanctuary of First Baptist Church.

First Baptist Church, Meridian, in the late 1930s.

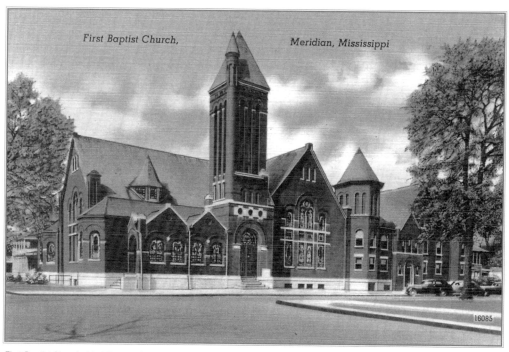

First Baptist Church, Meridian, as shown on a postcard from the 1940s.

The proposed design for the second Temple Beth Israel in Meridian.

Temple Beth Israel, Meridian, in the late 1930s.

Temple Beth Israel (II)

Meridian, Lauderdale County (1906)

The second Temple Beth Israel in Meridian was a Neoclassical building of brick construction, with a projecting portico of four unfluted columns in the Roman Ionic order. The building was capped by a dome raised upon a cylindrical drum on an octagonal base. It was built in 1906 at the northeast corner of Twenty-fourth Avenue and Eleventh Street, and was dedicated on December 14, 1906.[137] The architect was Penn Jeffries Krouse of Meridian,[138] who designed many other notable buildings in east-central and southeast Mississippi, including First Presbyterian Church in Meridian,[139] the Meridian City Hall, the twin Jones County Courthouses in Laurel and Ellisville, the old Newton County Courthouse in Decatur, the Clarke County Courthouse in Quitman, the Kemper County Courthouse in DeKalb, the Pearl River County Courthouse in Poplarville, and numerous public schools.[140] The temple was built by C. H. Dabbs and Company of Meridian,[141] who also worked with Krouse on Stephenson School in Meridian and the old Newton County Courthouse.

Along with the synagogues in Natchez (1904–5) and Greenville (1906),[142] Temple Beth Israel was one of the earliest examples of Neoclassical Revival religious architecture in Mississippi. Neoclassical Revival architecture gained widespread popular attention at the World's Columbian Exposition in Chicago in 1893, and was becoming fashionable for institutional buildings in northern cities by the mid-1890s, but it did not become popular in Mississippi until the completion of the New Capitol in 1903.

The Beth Israel congregation moved to their present synagogue complex in 1964, and the old temple was subsequently demolished.

Pine Ridge Presbyterian Church

North of Natchez, Adams County (1828)

Located on Pine Ridge Road, about seven miles north of downtown Natchez, the old Pine Ridge Presbyterian Church was built in 1828, replacing an earlier log church. It was a rectangular, gable-roofed brick church with round-arched windows and a central round-arched front door on the gable end. It was destroyed by a tornado in 1908 and was subsequently replaced by the present building on the same site. The adjacent session house, built in 1829, still stands.[143]

Clear Creek Baptist Church

Washington, near Natchez, Adams County (1828)

Built in 1828, the same year as Pine Ridge Presbyterian Church, Clear Creek Baptist Church at Washington, a short distance east of Natchez, was a rectangular Federal style brick church with round-arched windows and a central round-arched front door.[144] The Mississippi Baptist Convention was organized here in 1836.

The congregation was disbanded in the 1880s. The building stood vacant for many years and was eventually demolished.

First Baptist Church

New Albany, Union County (1898–99)

The old First Baptist Church in New Albany, built in 1898–99, was a Gothic Revival church of brick construction that stood at the south corner of Bankhead Street and Camp Street, across Camp Street from the Union County Courthouse. The design of the building seems likely to have been a local builder's adaptation of plans originally drawn up by Benjamin D. Price.[145] Certain details of the building that differ from Price's design, such as the ornamentation in the gables and the shape of the muntins and pattern of glass in the windows, are very similar to those on the old First Methodist Church of Booneville (see page 22), located about thirty-five miles away, suggesting that both churches were erected by the same builder.

In 1923–24 the old church was replaced on the same site by the present building of First Baptist Church.

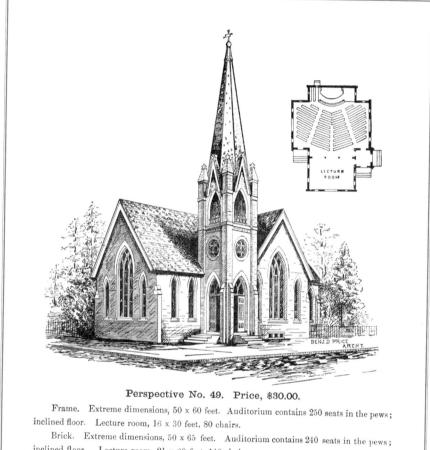

Perspective No. 49. Price, $30.00.

Frame. Extreme dimensions, 50 x 60 feet. Auditorium contains 250 seats in the pews; inclined floor. Lecture room, 16 x 30 feet, 80 chairs.

Brick. Extreme dimensions, 50 x 65 feet. Auditorium contains 240 seats in the pews; inclined floor. Lecture room, 21 x 30 feet, 110 chairs.

Brick. Extreme dimensions, 54 x 70 feet. Auditorium contains 310 seats in the pews; inclined floor. Lecture room, 19 x 34 feet, 110 chairs

Rooms connect by folding doors or rolling partitions; heated by furnace in cellar; walls, 16 feet; ceiling, 25 feet high. Tower, 10 x 10 feet, 70 feet high.

Approximate cost, $4000 to $5500.

72

The design of the old First Baptist Church of New Albany seems likely to have been based, in part, on this plan by Benjamin D. Price.

First Methodist Church
(Methodist Episcopal Church, South)

Newton, Newton County (circa 1900–4)

Most of the more prominent churches built in Mississippi's larger communities from the 1880s until about 1910 were built in a single, fairly consistent stylistic vocabulary, usually either Gothic Revival or Romanesque Revival, but there were also many churches that combined features from two or more different styles. The old First Methodist Church in Newton, built sometime between about 1900 and 1904, was an interesting combination of several styles. Its large front window and the lancet windows on the second tier of its front corner tower had Gothic arches, but the main doorway at the base of the tower and the window at the top of the tower had round-arched openings that were more Romanesque in character. The circular window in the upper façade could also be considered Romanesque, but the pattern of its muntins is Colonial Revival, and the incongruous little porch is adorned with wooden spindlework typical of the Queen Anne style.

First Baptist Church

Newton, Newton County (1908)

The second building of First Baptist Church in Newton, built in 1908, was a wood-frame auditorium-plan building with three broad, square corner towers. It was designed in a simplified Gothic style, with wide Tudor arches on the main windows.

In 1950 this building was replaced on the same site by the present, third building.

First Baptist Church, Oxford, as it appeared circa 1915–20, after the brick walls had been stuccoed.

First Baptist Church

Oxford, Lafayette County (1881–82)

The old First Baptist Church of Oxford was a late Victorian Gothic Revival church of brick construction located at the northwest corner of South Ninth Street (originally Warren Street) and Van Buren Avenue.[146] It was begun in 1881 and was dedicated on May 7, 1882.[147] An annex was built in 1910, at which time the building was stuccoed.[148]

In 1950, the congregation relocated to a new building across the street to the south, at 800 Van Buren Avenue, and the old sanctuary was subsequently demolished. Its site is now a parking lot for the present church.

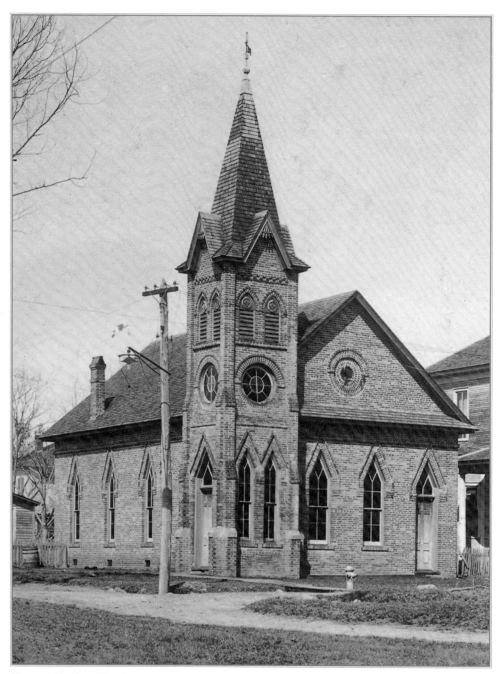

The second building of First Presbyterian Church in Pascagoula.

First Presbyterian Church (II)

Pascagoula, Jackson County (1896)

The original building of First Presbyterian Church in Pascagoula was a wood-frame structure, built in 1891, that stood at the northwest corner of Canty and Convent streets. It was destroyed by a fire in January 1896,[149] and was replaced later that year by a Gothic Revival brick building erected on the same site.[150] The doors and windows of the second church had steeply peaked openings instead of the more customary curved Gothic arches, but the louvered openings in the upper part of the corner tower did have curved Gothic arches.

In October 1955 the congregation relocated to the present First Presbyterian Church complex at the corner of Pascagoula Street and Ingalls Avenue. The old church on Canty Street remained standing until 1965, when it was demolished to clear the site for the construction of the Jackson County Chancery Court building.[151]

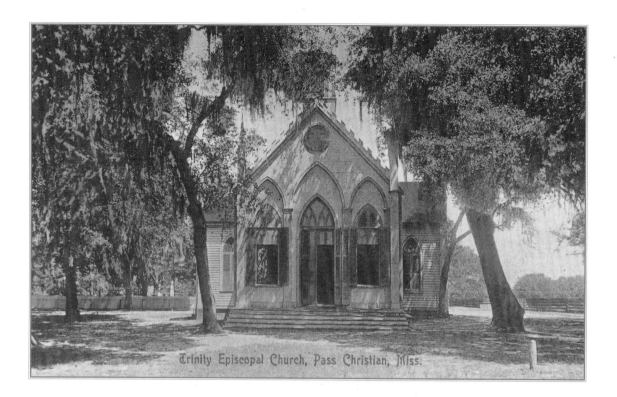

Trinity Episcopal Church, Pass Christian, Miss.

Trinity Episcopal Church

Pass Christian, Harrison County (circa 1849)

Many of the Gothic Revival churches erected in Mississippi during the antebellum period were surprisingly ornate buildings of wood-frame construction, particularly those built for Episcopal and Catholic congregations. One of the most elaborate of these Carpenter Gothic churches was Trinity Episcopal Church in Pass Christian, which was built about 1849.

This church was a richly detailed Carpenter Gothic building with a cross-shaped plan. The Gothic-arched door at the center of the front façade was flanked by Gothic-arched windows, all set within three slightly recessed Gothic-arched panels. The vergeboards along the top of the wall were trimmed with decorative battlements. Atop the roof ridge was a small square belfry. The interior of the church featured an impressive open-beamed ceiling framed with elaborate wood trusses.

This charming antebellum building, which had stood for 120 years, was destroyed by Hurricane Camille on August 17, 1969. It was replaced, on the same site, by a new building of simpler design. The second building was destroyed by Hurricane Katrina in 2005.

INTERIOR, TRINITY CHURCH.

This early twentieth-century postcard showed both the interior and the exterior of Trinity Episcopal Church.

St. Paul's Catholic Church, Pass Christian, as pictured on an early twentieth-century postcard.

St. Paul's Catholic Church

Pass Christian, Harrison County (1879)

Built in 1879, the old St. Paul's Catholic Church in Pass Christian was a Carpenter Gothic church with a center front tower capped by an octagonal spire. It had three entrances, one in the base of the tower and one at either side. It was located on Front Street (later Scenic Drive) just west of St. Paul Avenue.[152]

Old St. Paul's was destroyed by Hurricane Camille on August 17, 1969. It was replaced by a new building on the same site.

Carolina Presbyterian Church

Southwest of Philadelphia, Neshoba County (1842)

Carolina Presbyterian Church, located near Dowdville, about sixteen miles southwest of Philadelphia in rural Neshoba County, was organized in 1841. The original building, a simple rectangular wood-frame church with twin entrances, was believed to have been built in 1842.

This building was destroyed by a tornado in March 1966.[153] The congregation subsequently built a new building nearby, and is still active.[154]

First Baptist Church

Philadelphia, Neshoba County (1926)

The old First Baptist Church in Philadelphia was one of the many Neoclassical auditorium-plan churches built in Mississippi in the 1920s. Built in 1926 at the northwest corner of Pecan Avenue and East Myrtle Street,[155] it was a large brick building on a raised brick basement, with a two-story fenestration and a shallow Ionic portico that did not shelter the entrances, which were on either side of the portico. It was similar in design to the First Baptist Church in Biloxi (1924) (see page 21) and the First Baptist Church of McComb (1923–24) (see page 138), although those buildings had hexastyle (six-column) porticoes where the smaller Philadelphia church had a tetrastyle (four-column) portico.

It was later replaced on the same site by the present First Baptist Church building.

Zion Baptist Church, near Pontotoc, photographed for the WPA in the late 1930s.

Zion Baptist Church

Pontotoc vicinity, Pontotoc County

Like the old Presbyterian Church that once stood at Buena Vista in Chickasaw County (see page 30), the old Zion Baptist Church in the Zion community east of Pontotoc, in Pontotoc County, was a simple rectangular vernacular church of wood-frame construction, with two tiers of windows. Just from seeing a photograph of the exterior, a viewer may often find it difficult to determine if a building of this form contained two full stories or if it was of the old meeting house type containing one large, open interior space with balconies along the interior side walls. In this case, it seems likely that this was a two-story building, because at the far end of the side wall shown in the photograph, past the door in the center of the wall, is another door with steps leading to it, which probably opened to a staircase going directly upstairs. Typically, when buildings of this shape were of two full stories, the upper story served as a meeting hall for a fraternal lodge or some other organization, and a separate external door allowed members of the organization to reach their meeting area without entering the space used by the church downstairs.

It was later replaced by the present building of Zion Baptist Church.

Toxish Baptist Church (III) (1905)

Near Pontotoc, Pontotoc County

The simple rectangular church building, with a gabled roof and twin entrances on the gable end, remained a widely popular design for rural churches in Mississippi for many, many years, from the 1830s or earlier through the first decade of the twentieth century. A good example that dated from the early twentieth century was the third building of Toxish Baptist Church in Pontotoc County, which was built in 1905 for a church that had been founded in 1837. When photographed for the WPA in the late 1930s, it was completely unchanged from the time of its construction. It was a wood-frame building with a pair of matching single-leaf

The interior of Toxish Baptist Church in the late 1930s.

doors, without transoms, in the gabled front wall. Along the right-hand side wall were five four-over-four double-hung sash windows, and on the left-hand wall were four windows and a side door.

The WPA photo of the interior of the church shows the plank walls and ceiling, the simple, austere furnishings, and the stove that provided heat.

This building was moved aside in 1966 to allow room for the construction of a new sanctuary in the same location. Sometime later, the older building was demolished.

Magnolia Baptist Church
("Old Magnolia Church")

Near Port Gibson, Claiborne County (circa 1845–50?)

Apparently built in the 1840s or 1850s, Old Magnolia Church near Port Gibson was a traditional rectangular vernacular church of wood construction, with twin double-leaf front doors. The front façade was embellished by a round-arched center window, in an arrangement similar to that of nearby Rocky Springs Methodist Church.[156]

Old Magnolia Church was located on the old Rodney Road about five miles west of Port Gibson, not far from the Bruinsburg Landing on the Mississippi River. On April 30 and May 1, 1863, Union general Ulysses S. Grant landed his forces at Bruinsburg to begin his march toward Vicksburg. In what became known as the Battle of Port Gibson, fighting erupted near Old Magnolia Church as Confederate forces attempted to block the advance of the Union army. The church building survived the battle that raged around it, but for many years afterwards it bore scars from the fighting.

The building remained standing through the 1930s but was eventually destroyed. Its site is now commemorated by a marker interpreting its role in the Battle of Port Gibson.

First Baptist Church

Ripley, Tippah County (1916)

More than a dozen churches in Mississippi between 1910 and 1920 were Neoclassical churches with a distinctive, diagonally symmetrical quarter-round plan, designed by the architect J. E. Greene of Birmingham. Most of the churches of this type, including the old First Methodist Church in Amory (see page 10), the old First Baptist Church of Columbia (see page 43), and the old Baptist Church in Louisville (see page 126), were two stories in height and had a pair of monumental tetrastyle (four-column) porticoes, but there were at least three churches in Mississippi that were smaller, one-story versions of the same general design. One of these was the building erected for First Baptist Church in Ripley in 1916, which stood at the northeast corner of Main Street and Mulberry Street. It was very similar to the old First Baptist Church in Iuka (not extant), built in 1915 (see page 91), and Chalybeate Baptist Church in Tippah County (still active), built in 1918. Like both of those churches, it had a semi-recessed three-column portico on both of its two diagonally symmetrical façades.

The old Baptist Church at Ripley was demolished circa 1956 and was replaced by a new building on the same site.

Presbyterian Church

Scooba, Kemper County (circa 1895–1900)

Another of the numerous churches in Mississippi built from the mail-order plans of Benjamin D. Price was the Presbyterian Church at Scooba in Kemper County. Probably built around 1895–1900, it appears to have been built from one of the plans pictured as "Perspective Nos. 183, 183A, and 183C" in the 1906 edition of Price's *Church Plans*, though careful comparison of the photograph and the perspective drawing will reveal slight differences—the spire, as built, has four faces instead of eight, and the building has a wainscot of vertical flushboard siding across the front.

The building no longer stands.

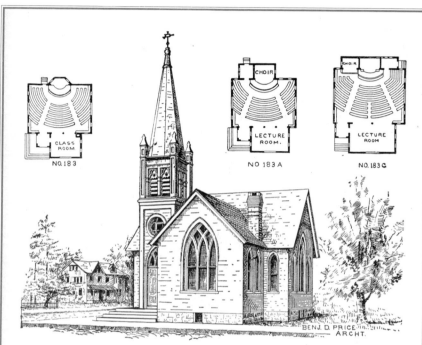

Perspective Nos. 183, 183A and 183C. Price, $20.00.

Nos. 183 and 183A. 32 x 40 feet, 200 seats; 32 x 45 feet, 230 seats; 32 x 50 feet, 260 seats. Prepared in brick or frame.

No. 183. Choir is seated in the front pew. Class room, 15 x 20 feet, 50 chairs.

No. 183A. Lecture room, 15 x 24 feet, 60 chairs. Rear extension, containing choir recess and pastor's room, 8½ x 23 feet.

No. 183C. 34 x 45 feet, 270 seats; inclined floor. Prepared in frame only. Lecture room, 18 x 30 feet, 95 chairs. Rear extension, containing choir recess, pulpit recess and pastor's room, 7 x 36 feet.

No. 183C. 33 x 51 feet, 260 seats; inclined floor. Prepared in brick veneer only. Lecture room, 15 x 25 feet, 60 chairs. Rear extension containing choir recess, pulpit recess and pastor's room, 9 x 49 feet.

Rooms connect by folding doors or rolling partitions. Heated by furnace in cellar. Walls, 14 feet. Ceiling, 20 feet high. Tower, 9 x 9 feet, 68 feet high.

Approximate cost, $2000 to $3500.

Please read pages 2 and 3.

53

"Perspective Nos. 183, 183A, and 183C" from *Church Plans* by Benjamin D. Price and Max Charles Price (1906).

First Methodist Church
(Methodist Episcopal Church, South)

Senatobia, Tate County (1880)

Built about 1880,[157] the old First Methodist Church of Senatobia stood on the north side of Gilmore Street facing eastward toward the Illinois Central Railroad. It was a noteworthy example of High Victorian Romanesque religious architecture, featuring round-arched windows with prominent hood-moldings, bands of

The old First Methodist Church of Senatobia, after the spire had been removed and replaced by an open belfry.

corbelled blind-arcading in the upper surfaces of all of the exterior walls, and a semiprojecting center-front tower that was surmounted by a broach spire. After the building was seriously damaged by a fire in 1932, the spire was replaced with a flat-topped, cubical open belfry.

The architect has not been identified, but it is possible that the building may have been designed by James B. Cook, a native of London, England, who practiced architecture in Memphis. Cook was the architect of the most prominent landmark building in Senatobia, the Tate County Courthouse, a High Victorian Romanesque building that was erected in 1875–76. Cook designed several Carpenter Gothic churches in north Mississippi for Episcopal congregations, including Holy Innocents in Como (1872)[158] and the Church of Our Savior in Iuka (1873).[159] He was probably also the architect of the Episcopal Church of the Redeemer in Sardis (1879), which no longer survives.

The old First Methodist Church was replaced by the present sanctuary, which was built across Gilmore Street to the south. It was begun in 1955 and dedicated in 1961. The site of the old church is currently used for parking.

The Methodist Episcopal Church, Shelby.

Perspective No. 141B. Price, $15.00. Brick.

Auditorium, 32 x 45 feet, 230 seats. Lecture room, 20 x 24 feet, 85 chairs.
Rear extension, containing choir recess, pulpit recess and pastor's room, 7 x 34 feet.

Rooms connect by rolling partitions or folding doors. Heated by furnace in cellar. Walls, 14 feet. Ceiling, 25 feet high. Finished in paneled and decorated wood work. Inclined floor. Tower, 10 x 10 feet, 57 feet high.

Approximate cost, $3800.

The old Shelby Methodist Church was built from the plan pictured as Perspective No. 141B in the 1906 edition of *Church Plans* by Benjamin D. Price and Max Charles Price.

Shelby Methodist Church
(Methodist Episcopal Church, South)

The First Methodist Episcopal Church, South, in Shelby, built in 1912, was one of the many churches built from mail order plans designed by Benjamin D. Price. It was built from the plan pictured as Perspective No. 141B in the 1906 edition of *Church Plans* by Benjamin D. Price and Max Charles Price. The church stood at the southeast corner of East Railroad Avenue (later Broadway) and Fourth Avenue.

The old church was replaced by a new building about 1949-50.[160]

First Presbyterian Church

Starkville, Oktibbeha County (1855)

Built in 1855, the old First Presbyterian Church in Starkville was an elegant temple-form Greek Revival church in the Doric order, of wood construction, elevated upon a full-story raised brick basement. Sheltering the entrance was a beautifully crafted tetrastyle portico of fluted Doric columns. It stood at the site of the present church, on the north side of Main Street west of Jackson Street.

This building was replaced in 1925–26 by the present sanctuary of First Presbyterian Church.[161]

Crawford Street Methodist Church

Vicksburg, Warren County (1846)

It was not uncommon in the 1840s and 1850s for churches to be built with a combination of Greek Revival and Gothic Revival features. Notable surviving churches of this type in Mississippi include the old St. Joseph's Catholic Church ("Church of the Yellow Fever Martyrs") (originally the first building of Christ Episcopal Church) in Holly Springs (circa 1840–42), Fredonia Methodist Church near Como in Panola County (1848), the Baptist Church at Rodney (circa 1850), and St. Mark's Episcopal Church in Raymond (1854).[162]

An interesting lost example of this combination of styles was the original building of Crawford Street Methodist Church in Vicksburg. Built in 1846, it stood at the southwest corner of Crawford and Cherry streets, facing north toward Crawford Street. A rectangular building of brick construction, it was distinguished by Greek Revival pediments on the front and rear façades and a classical cornice on all four walls. On the front and side walls were pointed Gothic windows. Surmounting the roof was a tall, square steeple (which was later removed).

This building stood during the siege of Vicksburg in 1863, and, like the Presbyterian Church (see page 183), was struck by Union artillery. This original building was demolished in 1899[163] to make room for the construction of the second building of the church (see page 188), which was built in 1899.

The original building of Crawford Street Methodist Church, probably photographed during the winter of 1898–99, shortly before its demolition. The steeple had been removed by this time.

The first Crawford Street Methodist Church being demolished early in 1899.

Catholic Church, Vicksburg, Miss.

St. Paul's Catholic Church

Vicksburg, Warren County (circa 1850)

St. Paul's Catholic Church in Vicksburg was built about 1850. An impressive Gothic Revival building, it was nearly identical in design to St. Mary's Cathedral (now St. Mary's Basilica) in Natchez.[164] Both churches were based on the design of St. Alphonsus Catholic Church in Baltimore, Maryland, which was the mother church of the Redemptorist order, to which Bishop William Henry

St. Mary's Basilica in Natchez, built from 1842 to 1859. St. Paul's in Vicksburg was nearly identical to St. Mary's.

St. Alphonsus Catholic Church in Baltimore, Maryland.

Elder belonged. Both churches are thought to have been designed by Robert Cary Long, Jr., of Baltimore, who was the architect of St. Alphonsus,[165] but apparently the two Mississippi churches had different supervising architects, at least initially. St. Paul's was built under the supervision of the firm of Logan & Warner,[166] while St. Mary's was begun by James Hardie in 1842 and completed by Peter Warner in 1859.

St. Paul's was severely damaged by the tornado that devastated downtown Vicksburg on December 5, 1953. It was demolished soon thereafter and was subsequently replaced by the present building on the same site.

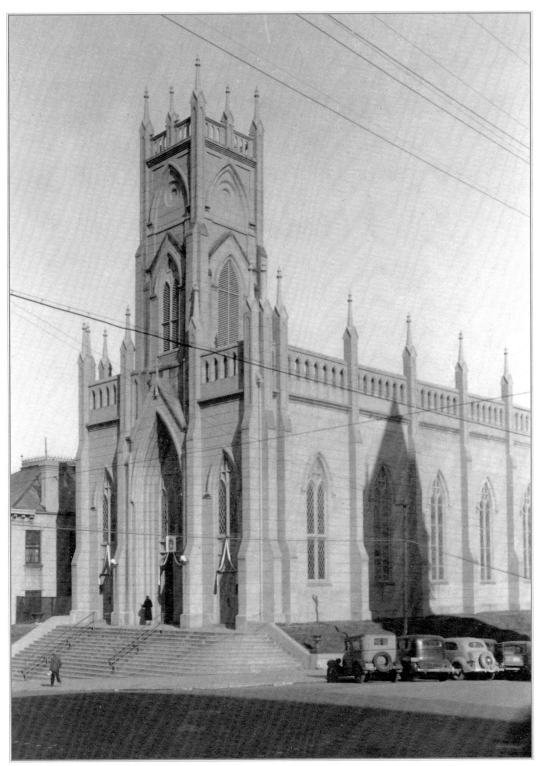

St. Paul's Catholic Church, Vicksburg, in the late 1930s. Its spire had been removed by then.

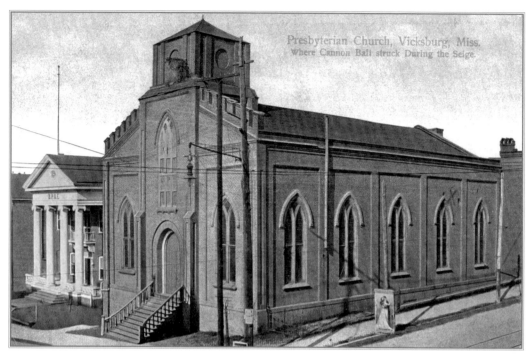

The old First Presbyterian Church of Vicksburg, as it appeared on a postcard about 1907.

First Presbyterian Church

Vicksburg, Warren County (1855)

Built in 1855 by local contractor Reynolds Clarke,[167] the old First Presbyterian Church of Vicksburg stood at the northeast corner of Clay and Walnut streets, which was later the site of the Hotel Vicksburg. The church was a rectangular gable-roofed brick building, three bays wide and five bays long, designed in a simplified Gothic Revival style, with a short, integral tower at the center of the front façade, surmounted by a shallow pyramidal roof. The building stood during the siege of Vicksburg in 1863, and bore a scar from the impact of a cannonball (which is visible, in the photograph, near the top of the fourth window from the left, marked by an "x").

This building was destroyed by fire on January 20, 1908 (as was the old Elks Lodge Hall next door), just as the present First Presbyterian Church on Cherry Street was nearing completion.[168] A newspaper article written soon after the fire described the durable construction of the building:

In tearing down the old heavy brick walls of the Presbyterian Church, which was destroyed by fire Monday morning, builders note with much interest the fact that this building of many years standing was among those that was [sic] put up with durability evidently the chief consideration. Instead of the eighteen and twenty inch wall of this day and time [1908], these walls were nearer thirty inches, and so well put up that they would doubtless have gone on for many more years, had not the fire done its part to cause the demolition of the structure.[169]

First Baptist Church, Vicksburg, before its extensive remodeling in 1906. This is a view northeastward from the tower of the old post office (later the Mississippi River Commission Building). The old Warren County Courthouse is visible in the distance.

First Baptist Church

Vicksburg, Warren County (1878–79, 1906–7)

The second building of First Baptist Church in Vicksburg was constructed in 1878–79, replacing an earlier building that had burned on March 21, 1878. It stood at the northwest corner of Walnut and Crawford streets, across Walnut Street from St. Paul's Catholic Church. In its original form it was a rectangular, hip-roofed brick building with Gothic arched windows and Classical Revival pilasters. At the southwest corner was a square corner entrance tower topped by a tall, slender spire.

From August 1906 until March 1907, the building was enlarged and extensively remodeled, to the extent that it appeared to be a different building, although a careful comparison of photographs of the structure before and after the remodeling will show that it was, in fact, the same building.

This building was seriously damaged by a fire in November 1956. Thereafter the congregation met at Grove Street School until the completion of the present sanctuary, at 1607 Cherry Street, in July 1958.[170]

First Baptist Church, Vicksburg, as it appeared in the 1930s. After its extensive remodeling in 1906, the building bore little resemblance to its earlier design, but a careful examination of the photographs reveals that it was, in fact, the same building. In both photographs, notice the small triangular window above the door, and, higher up, the two small lancet ventilators. The tall, slender windows in the walls were also original, but were freely repositioned.

Bethel African Methodist Episcopal Church

Vicksburg, Warren County (1879)

Bethel African Methodist Episcopal (A.M.E.) Church in Vicksburg was organized in 1864. In the late 1860s the congregation purchased a small wood-frame building at the southeast corner of Monroe Street and First East Street that had been the original building of First Presbyterian Church.[171] In 1879 the original building was replaced by a Gothic Revival building of brick construction.[172]

This church was demolished about 1911–12 to make room for the construction of the present third building of Bethel A.M.E. Church, which was erected on this same site in 1912.

Crawford Street Methodist Episcopal Church (II)

Vicksburg, Warren County (1899)

After the first building of Crawford Street Methodist Episcopal Church (see page 177) was demolished in 1899, construction began on a new building for the church on the same site, although the main façade of the new church faced east, toward Cherry Street, instead of north toward Crawford Street. The second building of Crawford Street Methodist Episcopal Church was a brick Gothic Revival auditorium-plan church that contained curved seating on a diagonal axis. Designed by W. A. Cann of St. Louis, Missouri,[173] it was a mirror image of Grace Methodist Church (1903) in Dallas, Texas, and First Presbyterian Church in Gainesville, Texas, both of which were also designed by Cann.

According to Sanborn fire insurance maps, an "institutional annex," containing a gymnasium, had been added at the southwest corner of the building by 1913.

The church burned on April 5, 1925,[174] and was replaced by the present sanctuary of Crawford Street United Methodist Church on the same site.[175]

The second building of Crawford Street Methodist Episcopal Church, as it appeared soon after its completion.

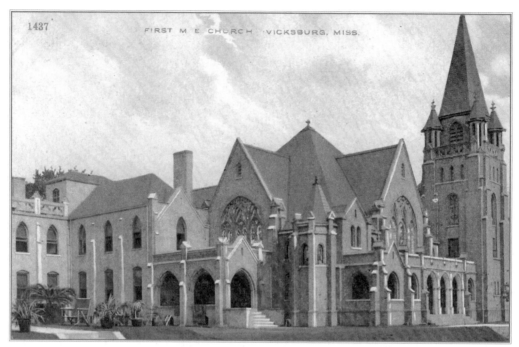

This postcard image of the second Crawford Street Methodist Episcopal Church shows the annex that had been added on the south side by 1913.

First Presbyterian Church of Gainesville, Texas is a mirror image of the second Crawford Street Methodist Episcopal Church. (The arcaded porch is barely visible on the right side in this photograph.)

Grace Methodist Church of Dallas, Texas, is also a mirror image of the second Crawford Street Methodist Episcopal Church.

The ruins of Crawford Street Methodist Episcopal Church, shortly after its destruction by fire on April 5, 1925. This photograph shows the steel framework that supported the roof over the auditorium.

Church of the Nativity (Episcopal)
(originally the Cumberland Presbyterian Church)

Water Valley, Yalobusha County (circa 1895, 1918)

Formerly located at 613 North Main Street, on the west side of Main Street on the third lot south of Clay Street, in Water Valley, this building was originally the Cumberland Presbyterian Church. It was built about 1895 from plans drawn up by Benjamin D. Price of Atlantic Highlands, New Jersey.[176] The same design was used for numerous other churches throughout the United States including the Methodist churches in Tarpon Springs, Florida; Grantville, Georgia;

Galeton, Pennsylvania; and Salado, Texas, but these churches were all built entirely of wood. The intricacy of the detailing of the Water Valley church suggests that the elaborate brickwork was original to the building, not a later veneer.

In 1918 the building was purchased and remodeled by the Episcopal congregation of the Church of the Nativity, to replace their earlier house of worship that had been located a half-block to the north, on the northwest corner of Main and Clay streets.[177] On November 1, 1918, the former Cumberland Presbyterian Church building was consecrated as the Church of the Nativity.[178]

This building was destroyed by a tornado that struck Water Valley on April 21, 1984.[179] A new building for the Church of the Nativity was erected soon thereafter on the same site.

BENJAMIN D. PRICE,
ARCHITECT

Perspective Nos. 42 and 42A.   Price, $15.00.   Frame.

No. 42.   28 x 50 feet, 200 seats;   30 x 50 feet, 220 seats;   32 x 50 feet, 240 seats.   Walls, 14 feet.   Ceiling, 20 feet high.

No. 42A.   32 x 50 feet, 170 seats.   Class room, 12½ x 23 feet, 45 chairs.   Gallery, over class room, 70 seats.   Walls, 16 feet.   Ceiling, 22 feet high.   Heated by furnace in cellar.   Belfry, 8 x 8 feet, 53 feet high.

Approximate cost, $1500 to $2000.

The Church of the Nativity in Water Valley was obviously built from a plan prepared by Benjamin D. Price. This page from Price's *Church Plans* of 1906 indicates that designs 42 and 42A were for wood frame buildings, but the Water Valley church appears to have been constructed of brick. The plan is a mirror image of the design shown here.

First Baptist Church

West Point, Clay County (1888)

The old First Baptist Church of West Point was built at the southwest corner of West Broad Street and Court Street in 1888. It replaced an identical building that was built in 1885–86,[180] but was destroyed by fire on October 14, 1887.[181] "In 14 months' time a building superior to the first was erected on the same spot."[182] It was dedicated on December 16, 1888.[183]

    As originally built, the church had a single door at the center of the front façade and a window in the base of the tower. The building was later remodeled;

First Baptist Church, West Point, as it appeared in the late 1930s.

The old sanctuary of First Baptist Church, West Point, being demolished in 1985.

the original center door was changed to a window and two front corner entrances were added. A Sunday school annex was built in 1916–17.[184]

A new sanctuary was built adjacent to the older one in the early 1980s. In 1982 the old church was listed on the National Register of Historic Places as a component of the Court Street Historic District, but the attention and recognition were not enough to save the building. The old sanctuary and the education annex were both demolished in 1985.

Cumberland Presbyterian Church
(later First Presbyterian Church)

West Point, Clay County (1898)

This building, which stood on the north side of Broad Street between Division and Court streets in West Point, was built in 1898 as the Cumberland Presbyterian Church. Several blocks to the east, the First Presbyterian Church congregation in West Point, which was affiliated with the "southern" Presbyterian Church (the Presbyterian Church in the United States) met in a wood-frame building on East Broad Street near Calhoun Street. The two congregations merged in 1925, keeping the name First Presbyterian Church but meeting in the 1898 Cumberland Presbyterian Church building.

The building was a Romanesque Revival auditorium-plan church of brick construction. A quasi-octagonal cupola was positioned at the center of the roof, but the building had no tower or steeple. This building was very similar in plan and detailing to the First United Methodist Church in Decatur, Alabama, which was built about 1899; but unlike this building the church in Decatur has a spired tower at one of its corner entrances and it does not have a cupola.

First Presbyterian Church of West Point erected a new building on a different site in 1953. The following year the older building was sold to the Church of Christ. It served as their house of worship until 1974, when it was sold to the First Pentecostal Church, which only used it for a short time. It was demolished in 1978.

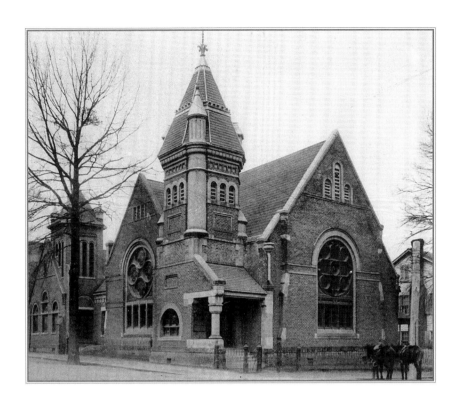

First Presbyterian Church

Yazoo City, Yazoo County (1887–88)

One of the most exuberant examples of Victorian Romanesque religious architecture ever built in Mississippi was the second building of First Presbyterian Church in Yazoo City, which was built in 1887–88 at the southwest corner of Broadway and West Main Street, replacing an earlier Presbyterian church which had stood on the same site. Sometime between July 1889 and February 1895 an addition was made to the south end of the building.

This building burned in the fire that destroyed downtown Yazoo City on May 25, 1904. It was replaced by the present building of First Presbyterian Church, which was built in 1905–6 two blocks to the northeast.[185]

First Baptist Church

Yazoo City, Yazoo County (1904)

After an earlier building on Washington Street was destroyed in the huge fire that devastated downtown Yazoo City on May 25, 1904, the congregation of First Baptist Church quickly constructed a substantial new building at the southwest corner of Broadway and Monroe Street. The new building appears on the Sanborn insurance map of Yazoo City that was made in January of 1905, only eight months after the fire. The new First Baptist Church was a Romanesque Revival auditorium-plan of brick construction. At its northeast corner was a square entrance tower that was topped by an ornate spire. An education building was added to the west of the sanctuary in 1926.

The congregation sold this building in 1956 and relocated to a new building at 328 Grand Avenue that was dedicated in 1957.[186] The Yazoo County Office Building was built on the site of the old church in 1958.

St. Stephen's Methodist Church
(Methodist Episcopal Church)

Yazoo City, Yazoo County (circa 1904)

St. Stephen's Methodist Church in Yazoo City has historically had an African American congregation. Their second building, built circa 1904, was a Gothic Revival church with a corner entrance tower that stood at the southeast corner of Jefferson Street and South Yazoo Street. It was replaced by a new building on the same site in 1959.

Notes

Factual information for which sources are not otherwise noted has largely been derived from the Historic Resources Inventory files of the Historic Preservation Division, Mississippi Department of Archives and History. Street address information up to about 1950 has largely been obtained from Sanborn fire insurance maps and, in Jackson, also from city directories.

1. Felix Lann and Carolyn Evans Sauter, *Methodism in Aberdeen: A Scrapbook of Historical Sketches from 1836 to 1957* (Aberdeen, Miss.: First United Methodist Church, 1986), p. 7.

2. The present building of First United Methodist Church is included in Sherry Pace, *Historic Churches of Mississippi*, essay and captions by Richard J. Cawthon (Jackson: University Press of Mississippi, 2007), p. 4.

3. "1888–1988 Centennial Program and History, First Baptist Church, Amory, Mississippi," p. 16.

4. In the 1970s, Washington Street was reconfigured as a loop around the north side of the central business district, and was later renamed Dr. Martin Luther King Jr. Boulevard. The site where the old Main Street Methodist Church formerly stood is now at the northeast corner of Dr. Martin Luther King Jr. Boulevard and Main Street, a block to the east of the Harrison County Courthouse.

5. It is referred to as a "false portico" because it does not project forward from the front wall far enough to actually function as a porch, although it is intended to look, from the front, like a conventional hexastyle portico.

6. This building was very similar to plan #220 on p. 105 of *Church Plans* by Benjamin D. Price and Max Charles Price (Atlantic Highlands, N.J.: privately published, 1906).

7. William L. Jenkins, *Mississippi United Methodist Churches* (Franklin, Tenn.: Providence House, 1998), p. 21.

8. Ibid., p. 26.

9. The present building of First United Methodist Church of Brookhaven is included in *Historic Churches of Mississippi*, p.13.

10. Inventory of Church Records (WPA), in the MDAH Archives.

11. Ibid.

12. "B'nai Israel Synagogue Has Stood Since 1877," *Madison County Herald*, November 8, 1973. The Mississippi Historical Records Survey (WPA), *Inventory of the Church and Synagogue Archives of Mississippi: Jewish Congregations and Organizations* (Jackson, Miss.: Mississippi State Conference, B'nai B'rith, 1940), p. 18, states incorrectly that the congregation was organized in 1877, the same year that the synagogue was built.

13. *Inventory of the Church and Synagogue Archives of Mississippi: Jewish Congregations and Organizations*, p. 18; and "B'nai Israel Synagogue Has Stood Since 1877." In Leo and Evelyn Turitz, *Jews in Early Mississippi* (Jackson, Miss.: University Press of Mississippi, 1983), p. 116, the date of construction of the synagogue is given as 1874.

14. The present First United Methodist Church of Canton is pictured in *Historic Churches of Mississippi*, p. 17.

15. "B'nai Israel Synagogue Has Stood Since 1877."

16. Letter from Elyda J. Garnett of Canton to P. Ana Gordon of the Historic Preservation Division, MDAH, dated February 3, 1983. The demolition of such a venerable building would be far less likely today. In 1989 the city of Canton adopted a historic preservation ordinance to protect historically and architecturally significant buildings from arbitrary destruction.

17. Inventory of Church Records (WPA), in the MDAH Archives.

18. Clarksdale Baptist Church is pictured in *Historic Churches of Mississippi*, p. 31.

19. First Baptist Church of Leland is pictured in *Historic Churches of Mississippi*, p. 76.

20. *Clarksdale Press Register*, January 9–10, 1982, p. 1. (Copy in the file on the old Christian Church in the Historic Resources Inventory files of the Historic Preservation Division, MDAH.)

21. Collins Baptist Church in the Historic Resources Inventory files, Historic Preservation Division, MDAH.

22. Sanborn fire insurance map of Collins, 1925.

23. College Hill Presbyterian Church is pictured in *Historic Churches of Mississippi*, p. 117.

24. Inventory of Church Records (WPA), in the MDAH Archives.

25. This famous church is illustrated in numerous books about English churches, including Simon Jenkins, *England's Thousand Best Churches* (London: The Penguin Press, 1999), pp.403–404.

26. The present First Baptist Church in Columbus is included in *Historic Churches of Mississippi*, p. 38.

27. This type of portico is often less accurately called a distyle-in-antis portico. The term "distyle" refers to a classical portico supported by two columns. A distyle-in-muris portico is a porch recessed behind the plane of a wall, fronted by two columns which are aligned with the plane of the wall. The term "distyle in antis" means an arrangement of two columns set within a recessed space between antae (projecting piers or pilasters). See K. Edward Lay, *The Architecture of Jefferson Country* (Charlottesville: University Press of Virginia, 2000), p. 333.

28. Government Street Presbyterian Church and Christ Church in Mobile are pictured in Mills Lane, *Architecture of the Old South: Mississippi and Alabama* (New York: Abbeville Press, 1989), pp. 53–55 and 59–60. Trinity Methodist Church in Savannah is pictured in Rita F. Spitler, *Higher Ground: Historic Churches and Synagogues in Savannah* (Savannah: T-Square Graphics, 1995), p. 50.

29. Jenkins, *Mississippi United Methodist Churches*, p. 49.

30. Mary Mariner Weaver, *And Are We Yet Alive? The Story of the Beginning and Progress of the Methodist Church in Corinth, Mississippi, 1799–1953* (Corinth, Miss.: First Methodist Church, 1955), p. 126.

31. Alcorn County Historical Association, *The History of Alcorn County* (1983), p.C-60.

32. *The Hundredth Anniversary of the First Baptist Church—The Highlights of One Hundred Years* (1955), p.10.

33. Ibid. The role of R. H. Hunt is not clearly documented. The booklet says, "D. A. Hunt [sic] from Chattanooga was architect either for this remodeling or for the building of the church in 1894." First Baptist Church in Corinth, Mississippi, is included on a list of R. H. Hunt Company plans that were in the collection of Selmon T. Franklin Associates of Chattanooga (a copy of which is in the files of the Historic Preservation Division, MDAH), but the nature of the work is not identified on that list. However, the building is not included on a very extensive list of buildings designed by R. H. Hunt that was published in the *Chattanooga Star* on August 31, 1907 (also in the files of the Historic Preservation Division, MDAH), which suggests that Hunt was the architect for the enlargement and remodeling, but not for the original design of the building.

34. From information accompanying the WPA photograph of the building, in the collections of MDAH. Nothing further is known about Callahan.

35. It closely resembles plan #220 on p. 105 and plan #216 on p. 90 of *Church Plans* by Benjamin D. Price and Max Charles Price (1906).

36. From the Web site of First Presbyterian Church of Corinth, viewed on September 19, 2007.

37. According to a handwritten note on the original paper copy of the 1925 Sanborn map for Drew, sheet 1, in the bound volume of Sanborn maps in the Historic Preservation Division collection.

38. Inventory of Church Records (WPA), in the collection of the MDAH Archives.

39. This building was somewhat similar to plan #109 on p. 46 of *Church Plans* by Benjamin D. Price and Max Charles Price.

40. Grace Episcopal Church in Carrollton, built in 1883, shared the same plan. It is included in *Historic Churches of Mississippi*, pp. 24–25.

41. Grace G. Everman and Lavinia D. Fort, eds., *History of St. James Church, Greenville, Mississippi, 1869–1946* (Greenville, Miss., 1946), pp. 15–16.

42. "Historic St. James to Start Moving Saturday," *Delta Democrat Times* (Greenville, Miss.), May 11, 1951. From a copy of the article in subject file "Episcopal Church, Greenville" at MDAH Library.

43. John T. Black, *Faith of Our Fathers: How Religion Has Influenced the History of Greenville, Mississippi* (Greenville, Miss., 2005), p. 33.

44. From a notation on the back of a WPA photo in the Historic Resources Inventory file at the Historic Preservation Division, MDAH.

45. Black, *Faith of Our Fathers*, p. 16.

46. Ibid.

47. Information provided via e-mail by Carol Holliger, Archivist, Archives of Ohio United Methodism, Ohio Wesleyan University, forwarded to the author by Diane Mallstrom, Reference Librarian, Genealogy & Local History/Cincinnati Room, Public Library of Cincinnati and Hamilton County, June 17, 2008.

48. Henry F. Withey and Elise Rathburn Withey, *Biographical Dictionary of American Architects (Deceased)* (1956; repr., Los Angeles: Hennessey and Ingalls, 1970), p. 147.

49. "Longtime vision becomes reality for First Baptist Church, members dedicate 13,000 square feet of additional space," *Daily Sentinel-Star* (Grenada, Miss.), Progress Edition, June 30, 1987, p. 12–C.

50. Sanborn insurance map of Grenada, Miss., 1925.

51. "Longtime vision becomes reality for First Baptist Church"; also J. B. Perry, Jr., "First Baptist Church—Serving Christ in Grenada" (1972), on the Web site of First Baptist Church, Grenada, viewed on January 19, 2008.

52. Hattiesburg Area Historical Society, *History of Forrest County* (Hattiesburg: Hattiesburg Area Historical Society, 2000), p. 39.

53. From information in the collections of the Diocesan Archives, Catholic Diocese of Jackson.

54. The old church is shown on the Sanborn insurance maps of Hattiesburg for 1910 (sheet 4), 1915 (sheet 17), 1925 (sheet 20), 1931 (sheet 24), and 1949 (sheet 24). The present church is shown on the Sanborn maps for 1931 (sheet 22), and 1949 (sheet 22).

55. From information in the collections of the Diocesan Archives, Catholic Diocese of Jackson.

56. The Sanborn insurance map of Hattiesburg, Miss., made in October 1906 (sheet 6) does not show the portion of Buschman Street where the building was located, but the church does appear on the Sanborn map of May 1910 (sheet 6). The building as remodeled in 1915 appears on the Sanborn map of August 1915 (sheet 3), May 1925 (sheet 13), April 1931 (sheet 5), and August 1949 (sheet 5).

57. E-mail correspondence from Laurie Crowson of the Hattiesburg Area Historical Society, August 31, 2008.

58. The church was not, however, included in an extensive list of works by R. H. Hunt that was published in the *Chattanooga Star* in 1907.

59. Moore Memorial Methodist Church in Winona is pictured in *Historic Churches of Mississippi*, p.160.

60. Inventory of Church Records (WPA), in the MDAH Archives.

61. Reagan L. Grimsley, *Hattiesburg in Vintage Postcards* (Charleston, S.C.: Arcadia Publishing, 2004), p. 60.

62. The Baptist Church, Hazlehurst, Mississippi, is included on a list of buildings designed by R. H. Hunt that was published in the *Chattanooga Star* on August 31, 1907.

63. The present building of First Baptist Church of Hazlehurst is included in *Historic Churches of Mississippi*, p.59.

64. The building is shown as a library on the 1943 update of the 1925 Sanborn insurance map of Hazlehurst.

65. Other examples of churches with the quarter-round plan are the old First Methodist Church in Amory (1914) (page 10), the old Baptist Church in Louisville (1915) (page 126), and the old First Baptist Church of Columbia (1911–12), (page 43).

66. William D. McCain, *The Story of Jackson: A History of the Capital of Mississippi, 1821–1951*, vol. 1 (Jackson, Miss.: J. F. Hyer Pub. Co., 1953), pp. 150–151.

67. Christ Church is documented in the *Inventory of the Church Archives of Alabama—Protestant Episcopal Church* (1939), pp. 24–25; *William Nichols, Architect* (1979), pp. 18, 41; *The Alabama Catalog: HABS* (1987), p. 352; and Lane, *Architecture of the Old South: Mississippi and Alabama*, p.47. Christ Church was later extensively remodeled.

68. McCain, *The Story of Jackson*, vol. 1, p.154.

69. Ibid., p.275.

70. A. S. Coody, in an account of the history of First Christian Church written in 1925, cited in McCain, *The Story of Jackson*, vol. 1, pp.159–160. Coody is also cited in Craig J. Lobb, *History of the First Christian Church of Jackson, Mississippi* (Jackson, Miss.: First

Christian Church, 1987), 5th page (not numbered). Lobb also cites another source that indicates that the building was standing by 1853.

71. Lobb, *History of the First Christian Church of Jackson, Mississippi*, 6th page.

72. McCain, *The Story of Jackson*, vol. 1, p. 198.

73. Ibid., pp.156–157.

74. Ibid., p. 268.

75. Ibid., p. 269.

76. Ibid.

77. The article is quoted at length in McCain, *The Story of Jackson*, vol. 1, p. 269.

78. The present St. Andrew's Episcopal Cathedral is pictured in *Historic Churches of Mississippi*, pp.64–65.

79. It has long been believed that there was an even earlier synagogue that was burned during the Civil War and was replaced by the one that burned in 1874. Recent research, however, has established that the first synagogue was not erected until after the Civil War.

80. An account of the dedication ceremony was quoted in Mary Carol Miller, *Lost Landmarks of Mississippi* (Jackson: University Press of Mississippi, 2002), p. 102.

81. The old Temple Anshe Chesed, which was vacated in 1969 and demolished in 1983, is included in Miller, *Lost Landmarks of Mississippi*, pp. 99–101. The strong similarity of the second Temple Beth Israel to the original design of Temple Anshe Chesed suggests that Joseph Willis might have been the architect of that building as well.

82. Galloway Memorial United Methodist Church is pictured in *Historic Churches of Mississippi*, p.68.

83. According to *The Episcopal Church in Mississippi, 1763-1992* (Jackson: The Episcopal Diocese of Mississippi, 1992), p. 85 and p. 99, Battle Hill, the second house on the site to serve as the bishop's residence, stood from 1877 until it burned on January 17, 1919. The house was replaced by a new dwelling on the same site, which served as the bishop's residence until 1950. The residence was located on land, originally 140 acres in extent, which had been acquired by the Episcopal Church in 1851. The property received its name in recognition of fighting that had taken place in the area during the Civil War.

84. Sanborn insurance map of Jackson, Mississippi, 1925 (sheet 38).

85. *The Episcopal Church in Mississippi, 1763–1992*, p. 59.

86. Both of these churches are pictured in *Historic Churches of Mississippi*, Grace Church on p. 115 and Church of the Resurrection on p. 143.

87. *The Episcopal Church in Mississippi, 1763–1992*, p. 60.

88. After its completion in 1903, St. Andrew's, as the largest church in the state's capital city, served for many years as a sort of de facto cathedral. It was formally designated as St. Andrew's Cathedral in 1966. See *The Episcopal Church in Mississippi, 1763–1992*, pp. 116–117. St. Andrew's is pictured in *Historic Churches of Mississippi*, pp.64–65.

89. *The Episcopal Church in Mississippi, 1763–1992*, p. 59, states, "With time the native stone deteriorated [and] was further weakened by fire and the building was demolished in 1919." Given the contradiction between that information and what is shown on the 1925 Sanborn map, and the fact that the Battle Hill house burned in 1919, it seems more likely that the chapel was burned in 1919, at the same time as the house, that it stood thereafter as a ruin until at least 1925, when it is shown as "dilapidated" on the Sanborn map (1925, sheet 38), and that it was finally demolished sometime after 1925.

90. Sanborn map of Jackson, Mississippi, November 1946 (sheet 38).

91. *The Episcopal Church in Mississippi, 1763–1992*, pp. 99–100.

92. Sanborn map of Jackson, Mississippi, April 1962, volume I, sheet 38, and Jackson city directory, 1955.

93. McCain, *The Story of Jackson*, vol. 1, p.271.

94. From the Web site of St. Columb's Episcopal Church, Ridgeland (www.stcolumbs.org), viewed on August 19, 2008.

95. Inventory of Church Records (WPA), in the collection of the MDAH Archives, and McCain, *The Story of Jackson*, vol. 1, p.275.

96. First Presbyterian Church, Jackson, Mississippi, is included on an extensive list of buildings designed by R. H. Hunt that was published in the *Chattanooga Star* (Chattanooga, Tenn.) on August 31, 1907.

97. The old Hazlehurst Baptist Church and the old First Baptist Church in Meridian are included in this book, on pages 90 and 144. The First United Methodist Church in Greenwood and the Moore Memorial United Methodist Church in Winona are included in *Historic Churches of Mississippi*.

98. McCain, *The Story of Jackson*, vol. 1, p.275.

99. Temple Gemiluth Chassed is included in *Historic Churches of Mississippi*, pp. 126–127.

100. From the Web site of First Presbyterian Church, Jackson, viewed on July 5, 2007.

101. The library later moved across State Street into the former Sears building, and was renamed the Eudora Welty Library. The old library served for a time as offices for the city of Jackson, but in recent years has stood vacant. It has recently been acquired by the Mississippi Baptist Convention and is slated for restoration.

102. The first building was the brick church built about 1845–50, included in this book on page 96. The second building was a wooden chapel that was erected about 1885, which was apparently intended to serve temporarily until a substantial brick building—the third building—could be erected.

103. The designer of the building is not documented. The building could have been designed by Taylor, or he may have built it according to plans drawn up by someone else.

104. Persons who are not well acquainted with late Victorian religious architecture, upon seeing photographs of this building, sometimes express surprise or puzzlement about the prominent Star of David visible in the large circular window on the west side, thinking that it must indicate that the building had been used as a Jewish synagogue. Actually, it was not all that uncommon for the Star of David to be used in late nineteenth-century churches. Many of the designs of Benjamin D. Price included the symbol as a window tracery design (though usually turned so that two of the sides are vertical), including the former Methodist Church in West Point, Mississippi, that is now the First Christian Church there. Another Mississippi church that has a prominent six-pointed star is the First Methodist Church in Lexington (pictured in *Historic Churches of Mississippi*, p. 82). First Baptist Church in Lexington also had a prominent six-pointed star, before it was extensively remodeled in 1929–30.

105. The addition appears on the 1914 Sanborn map (sheet 15). William D. McCain, in *The Story of Jackson*, vol. 1, p.280, wrote that "the building was not actually completed until 1912." This seems to be in error—the building was apparently completed, as initially planned, about 1893–94, but it was subsequently enlarged about 1912.

106. In 2002 the First Christian congregation moved out of that building and relocated to a much smaller building on Briarwood Drive.

107. It is now part of the Galloway Memorial United Methodist Church complex.

108. McCain, *The Story of Jackson*, vol. 1, p.259.

109. Ibid.

110. Richard Aubrey McLemore and Namie Pitts McLemore, *The History of First Baptist Church of Jackson, Mississippi* (Jackson: Hederman Brothers, 1976), pp. 77–78.

111. McLemore and McLemore, *History of First Baptist Church of Jackson*, p. 77.

112. McCain, *The Story of Jackson*, vol. 1, p.260.

113. Ibid.

114. Ibid., p.263.

115. Ibid., p.264.

116. The church is not shown on the Sanborn insurance map of Jackson, Miss., of 1914, but it is listed at that location in the Jackson city directory of 1916 and it is shown at that location on the Sanborn map of 1918 (sheet 27).

117. From the file on I. C. Garber in the architects and contractors files at the Historic Preservation Division, MDAH. Galloway Memorial United Methodist Church is pictured in *Historic Churches of Mississippi*, p. 68.

118. From the Web site of New Stage Theatre (www. newstagetheatre.com), viewed on May 1, 2008.

119. From the Web site of Temple Beth Israel, viewed on July 28, 2008.

120. Jimmy Bass (photography) and Nell Davis (text), *A Pictorial History of Laurel, Mississippi* (Laurel, Miss.: privately published, 1991), p.86.

121. Bass and Davis, *A Pictorial History of Laurel, Mississippi*, p.87.

122. The present sanctuary of First Presbyterian Church in Laurel is included in *Historic Churches of Mississippi*, p.69.

123. Since the mid-1970s, and particularly since the reunification of the northern and southern Presbyterian churches in 1983, there have been numerous changes in the affiliations of Mississippi's Presbyterian congregations. At the time this book was being prepared, the Louisville Presbyterian Church was affiliated with the Evangelical Presbyterian Church, while the First Presbyterian Church of Louisville was associated with the Presbyterian Church in America (PCA).

124. T. W. Crigler, ed., *History of the First Baptist Church, 1835–1960, Macon, Mississippi* (Macon: First Baptist Church, 1960), p. 134.

125. The third sanctuary of First Baptist Church in Macon is pictured in *Historic Churches of Mississippi*, pp. 86–87.

126. St. Mary's Episcopal Church in Lexington is pictured in *Historic Churches of Mississippi*, pp. 78–79.

127. B'nai Sholom Synagogue in Brookhaven is pictured in *Historic Churches of Mississippi*, p. 12.

128. J. B. Cain, *Magnolia Methodist Church, 1856–1956* (Nashville: Parthenon Press, 1961), pp. 56–57.

129. The present St. Alphonsus Catholic Church is included in *Historic Churches of Mississippi*, pp. 94–95.

130. It is referred to as a "false portico" because it does not project forward from the front wall far enough to actually function as a porch, although it is intended to look, from the front, like a conventional hexastyle portico.

131. Inventory of Church Records (WPA), in the MDAH Archives.

132. St. Paul's Episcopal Church is pictured in *Historic Churches of Mississippi*, p. 98.

133. *The Episcopal Church in Mississippi, 1763–1992*, p. 197.

134. The cornerstone was laid in on August 19, 1885, according to W. B. Jones, *Methodism in the Mississippi Conference, 1870–1894* (Jackson: Mississippi Conference Historical Society, 1951), p. 285.

135. Jenkins, *Mississippi United Methodist Churches*, p. 36.

136. First Baptist Church, Meridian, Mississippi, is included on the list of buildings designed by R. H. Hunt that was published in the *Chattanooga Star* (Chattanooga, Tenn.) on August 31, 1907.

137. Inventory of Church Records (WPA), in the MDAH Archives.

138. From the cornerstone, transcribed by Mrs. Lucile Lowry Lake in 1939 for the Inventory of Church Records (WPA). This documentation is on file in the MDAH Archives.

139. First Presbyterian Church in Meridian is pictured in *Historic Churches of Mississippi*, pp. 96–97.

140. All of these buildings are extant in 2009 except the old Newton County Courthouse.

141. From the cornerstone.

142. Both are pictured in *Historic Churches of Mississippi*.

143. The present Pine Ridge Presbyterian Church is pictured in *Historic Churches of Mississippi*, p. 108.

144. According to xerographic copies of photographs in the Historic Resources Inventory file for this building at the Historic Preservation Division, MDAH, this church had fine Federal Style detailing on the interior, but clear images of those photographs were not available for inclusion in this book.

145. This building was similar in appearance to plan #47 on page 72 of *Church Plans* by Benjamin D. Price and Max Charles Price, but the tower more closely resembled that of plan #220 on p. 105.

146. The church appears on the Sanborn maps of Oxford, Miss., 1890 (sheet 2), 1895 (sheet 2), 1900 (sheet 4), 1905 (sheet 4), 1910 (sheet 7), 1916 (sheet 7), 1925 (sheet 6), and 1948 (sheet 6).

147. From an article about the churches of Oxford at the Historic Preservation Division, MDAH in *The Oxford Eagle*, December 16, 1937 (copy in Historic Resources Inventory file for St. Peter's Episcopal Church, Oxford).

148. Inventory of Church Records (WPA), in the MDAH Archives.

149. Pascagoula *Democrat-Star*, Friday, January 17, 1896.

150. Information in the file on First Presbyterian Church at the Pascagoula Public Library. The location is shown on the Sanborn insurance maps of Pascagoula, Miss., 1904, 1918, 1924, and 1950. The church later relocated to 1819 Pascagoula Street.

151. Information in the file on First Presbyterian Church at the Pascagoula Public Library.

152. The building appears on the Sanborn maps of Pass Christian, Miss., 1893 (sheet 2), 1898 (sheet 2), 1904 (sheet 3), 1909 (sheet 3), 1918 (sheet 4), 1924 (sheet 5), 1930 (sheet 5), and 1948 (sheet 5).

153. Information from the Neshoba County "rootsweb" genealogy Web site, viewed on February 5, 2008.

154. Directory of churches, on the Web site of the Presbyterian Church in America, viewed on February 5, 2008.

155. This building appears on the Sanborn insurance maps of Philadelphia, Miss., 1932 (sheet 3) and 1942 (sheet 3).

156. Rocky Springs Methodist Church is pictured in *Historic Churches of Mississippi*, p. 132.

157. *Mississippi United Methodist Churches*, p. 177.

158. Holy Innocents Episcopal Church in Como is included in *Historic Churches of Mississippi*, pp. 40–41.

159. The Church of Our Savior in Iuka is included in *Historic Churches of Mississippi*, p. 63.

160. Ground was broken for the new building in 1949. "Shelby's First United Methodist Church celebrates its centennial," *Delta Democrat Times* (Greenville, Miss.), October 9, 1988.

161. The present sanctuary of First Presbyterian Church of Starkville is pictured in *Historic Churches of Mississippi*, p.145.

162. All four of these churches are featured in *Historic Churches of Mississippi*.

163. J. Allen Lindsey, *Methodism in the Mississippi Conference, 1894–1919* (Jackson: Mississippi Conference Historical Society,1964), p. 58.

164. St. Mary's Basilica in Natchez is pictured in *Historic Churches of Mississippi*, pp.102–103.

165. The author is indebted to James T. Wollon, Jr., AIA, of Havre de Grace, Maryland, for sharing this information.

166. Logan & Warner are credited as the architects of the church in an illustration of the building that appeared in the 1860 catalog of Hinkle, Guild & Co., a Cincinnati building supply company. There is a copy in the file for St. Paul's Catholic Church in the Historic Resources Inventory files of the Historic Preservation Division, MDAH.

167. From an article about the old Presbyterian Church in the *Vicksburg Daily Herald*, Friday, January 24, 1908, in the file on the Old Presbyterian Church at the Old Court House Museum in Vicksburg.

168. The present First Presbyterian Church is pictured in *Historic Churches of Mississippi*, p.154.

169. From an article about the old Presbyterian Church in the *Vicksburg Daily Herald*, Friday, January 24, 1908, cited above.

170. From a file on the old First Baptist Church in the library of the Old Court House Museum in Vicksburg.

171. First Presbyterian Church had moved to a brick Gothic church at the northeast corner of Clay and Walnut streets in 1855. That building is included in this book, on page 183.

172. Inventory of Church Records (WPA), in the MDAH Archives.

173. Lindsey, *Methodism in the Mississippi Conference, 1894–1919*, p. 34, credits the design of this building to W. A. Cann. The American Institute of Architects *Guide to Dallas Architecture* (1999) (p.43) shows Grace United Methodist Church (1903) of Dallas, Texas, to be a virtually identical mirror image of this church, and credits the design to W. A. Caan of St. Louis. Research on the Internet indicates that the correct spelling is Cann.

174. Gordon Cotton, "Crawford Street Methodist Church Evolved from Humble Beginnings," *Vicksburg Sunday Post*, October 14, 1984. From a copy of the article in the files of the Old Court House Museum, Vicksburg.

175. The present sanctuary of Crawford Street Methodist Church is pictured in *Historic Churches of Mississippi*, p.153.

176. This building was very similar in appearance to plans #42 and #42A on page 33 of *Church Plans* by Benjamin D. Price and Max Charles Price. The mail order plans of Benjamin D. Price are discussed in this book on page 28.

177. Both the Cumberland Presbyterian Church and the original Church of the Nativity appear on the 1910 Sanborn map of Water Valley (sheet 5).

178. *Inventory of the Church Archives of Mississippi—Protestant Episcopal Church—Diocese of Mississippi* (1940), pp. 91–92.

179. "Town Picks up the Pieces in Wake of Killer Storm," *Clarion-Ledger* (Jackson, Miss.), April 23, 1984.

180. It appears as "not completed" on the Sanborn map of November 1885 (sheet 2).

181. Tom Womack, *A History of the First Baptist Church of West Point, Mississippi, 1885–1985* (West Point, Miss.: Sullivan's Printing Company,1987), p. 16.

182. Ibid., p. 17.

183. Ibid.

184. Ibid., pp. 54–55.

185. The present building of First Presbyterian Church in Yazoo City is included in *Historic Churches of Mississippi*, p. 176.

186. *Yazoo County Story* (1958), p. 118.

Glossary

arcade; blind arcade

In formal architectural terminology, an *arcade* is a row of arches, or in some cases a porch or covered walkway placed behind a row of arches. The arches of an arcade are typically open, but in some instances a row of arches may be applied to the surface of a wall as decorative element (particularly in Romanesque or Romanesque Revival architecture), with only a solid wall within each arch, in which case it is said to be a *blind arcade*. In the design of Romanesque Revival churches, blind arcades are most typically applied in a miniature form underneath eaves, and particularly under the sloping or "raked" eaves of a gable-end wall. These are normally "corbelled" arches, which means arches made of bricks or stones that step outward from the wall; hence, a miniature arcade along the eaves of a Romanesque church is typically a **corbelled blind arcade**. (See *corbelling*.)The use of arcades as architectural features is called **arcading**.

auditorium; nave; sanctuary

In the terminology traditionally used to describe churches, particularly the medieval churches of England and France, the part of the interior of a church building where the congregation is assembled is called the *nave*. In this traditional terminology, the word *sanctuary* refers only to the **chancel**—the area immediately surrounding the altar. In some of the more highly liturgical churches these terms are still used in this way, particularly if the building is a "High Gothic"

church that carefully emulates medieval Gothic models. During the eighteenth and early nineteenth centuries, there was not any need for a particular word to describe the primary worship space within a church, because the architectural form of a church typically consisted of one structure that contained only one large room. In the latter part of the nineteenth century, churches began to have other interior spaces—lecture halls, Sunday school rooms, parish halls, etc., and it became useful to have a word that pertained specifically to the main worship space. Among evangelical churches the usual term to describe this space was *auditorium* (particularly after the introduction of the **auditorium-plan church**). Some denominations, particularly Presbyterians, preferred the word *sanctuary*, the meaning of which was expanded to include the entire worship space and the building that contained it, when there were other buildings in a complex. Both widely used today, the terms **sanctuary** and **auditorium** were both used in the late nineteenth century and the early twentieth century. In her book *When Church Became Theatre: The Transformation of Evangelical Architecture and Worship in Nineteenth-Century America*, Jeanne Halgren Kilde writes, "The terms *auditorium, audience room*, and *sanctuary* were all commonly used during the last third of the nineteenth century to designate the main worship room of evangelical churches. Adopting the term *sanctuary*, Congregationalists and Presbyterians indicated the extent to which the interest in liturgics and more

High Church worship forms popularized during the Gothic Revival period had achieved a lasting place in their religious symbol system" (note 3 on p. 249).

auditorium plan church

An *auditorium-plan church* is a church that is designed in such a way that its congregational seating area has the form of a theater, having a sloped floor and curved seating placed so that each seat has a good view of the pulpit or rostrum. The seating normally consists of pews arranged in concentric circular arcs, centered on the pulpit. Typically the pews are placed so that the center of the room, in front of the pulpit, is filled with seats, and the aisles radiate at angles off to either side, so that there is not a center aisle (much to the chagrin of modern-day wedding planners, who like to have a wide center aisle for the bride's procession).

The auditorium plan is sometimes mistakenly referred to as the **Akron Plan**. That term actually refers to an approach to the conducting of Sunday school classes that was promoted at the end of the nineteenth century and the beginning of the twentieth century that utilized a group of small classroom spaces that opened into a center auditorium, or sometimes into the main auditorium of the church. The term is also used to describe a church designed to accommodate this type of Sunday school; but it refers to the arrangement of classroom spaces opening into the auditorium, not to the design of the auditorium itself.

bay

A *bay*, in architecture, is the space between two regularly recurring structural elements, such as columns or structural posts, or an equivalent unit of distance that forms a proportional module in the overall design of the building. It is easiest to understand how the term is used by considering a building shaped like an ancient Greek temple, that has, for example, six columns across the front and back, and ten columns along either side. By counting the spaces between the columns, one can describe it as being five bays wide and nine bays long. When a building has a wall that is not articulated by columns or pilasters, it is sometimes described as if each regularly spaced window unit or doorway occupies a single bay, so that the old First Presbyterian Church in Vicksburg can be described as being three bays wide and five bays long. (One has to be careful in using the word, however, because it only has valid meaning when it is applied to regularly spaced features that provide a proportional rhythm to the building, not to just any doors and windows!)

broach spire (see *spire*)

chancel

In the terminology traditionally used to describe the medieval churches of England, the **chancel** is the part of the interior of a church building that contains the altar (or communion table) and often also the pulpit and lectern. In traditional usage, the chancel is distinct and visually separate from the **nave**, which is the large, open hall where the congregation is assembled. Churches that use a formal "liturgical" manner of worship, such as Episcopal and Catholic churches, tend to have a distinct chancel, in the traditional sense (although one of the effects of the Vatican II changes in the Catholic Church was to bring the altar out from the chancel and into the nave). In church buildings that are not designed for a traditional liturgical manner of worship, the term **chancel** is sometimes applied to the **rostrum** or raised platform where the pulpit is located, especially if it is a visually distinct space.

corbelling

Corbelling is a method of laying brickwork or stonework in which one or more bricks or stones in one course project slightly forward from the course below. Stacking up several of these projecting bricks or stones can be used to create brackets, arches, or decorative surface treatments such as a **corbelled blind arcade**. A projection made of bricks or stones laid this way is called a **corbel**.

Corinthian (see *order*)

cupola

A *cupola* is a vertical structure on the roof of a building. It is usually circular or octagonal in shape, and is typically capped by a small dome. A cupola on a church may contain a **belfry** (a chamber where a bell or a set of bells is hung) or it may contain windows so that it can serve as a "lantern" to provide light into the space below, particularly if it sits on top of a dome.

distyle (see *portico*)

distyle in antis (see *portico*)

distyle in muris (see *portico*)

Doric (see *order*)

fenestration

In formal architectural terminology, *fenestration* (from the Latin *fenestra*, "window") is the design and placement of windows (and doors) in a building. The pattern of fenestration is sometimes described in terms of **bays** (see *bay*). The fenestration can be a clue to the interior plan, but it can also be misleading, particularly because it is not unusual for a church to have an auditorium with two tiers of windows, one tier providing light to an interior balcony or side gallery and the other for the aisle or seating area below the balcony, resulting in a building that looks like it contains two distinct stories when actually its auditorium is a single large space. (For a discussion of the design of windows, see *windows*.)

gable; gablet

A *gable* is a triangle-shaped part of a wall that is located where the planes of a conventional two-slope pitched roof intersect the wall. On a simple rectangular building with a pitched (or "gabled") roof, the narrower end-walls topped by gables are sometimes called "gable ends" of the building. Small elements of the building that have their own exterior walls, particularly those that are located on the roof, such as dormer windows, may also have gables. A very small triangular feature that projects from or interrupts a major roof plane of the building is called a *gablet*.

Gothic; Gothic Revival

The term *Gothic* refers to the religious architecture of Western Europe in the late medieval period, from the twelfth through the fifteenth centuries or later. Medieval Gothic architecture was characterized by the use of pointed arches instead of the round arches used in earlier Romanesque architecture (see *Romanesque*).

Gothic architecture was revived in the late eighteenth and early nineteenth centuries as an architectural style called *Gothic Revival*. The earliest Gothic Revival architecture treated Gothic-inspired features as picturesque novelties, but by the 1840s there was a movement in the Episcopal and Catholic churches to revive Gothic architecture by careful emulation of medieval models. This movement is called the Ecclesiological Movement, and the style of religious architecture it produced is called "Ecclesiological Gothic." By the middle of the nineteenth century some of the more evangelical denominations had begun to adopt the Gothic Revival, and by the 1880s it was being used for churches of every major denomination. Some late nineteenth-century churches exhibited a distinctive approach to the style called "High Victorian Gothic," but many other churches (including many auditorium-plan churches) were designed in a very loose and freely interpreted version of Gothic. A variation of Gothic Revival religious architecture was developed for use in churches built of wood, which came to be called "Carpenter Gothic" or "Carpenters' Gothic." It was not unusual for late nineteenth-century churches to combine Gothic Revival and Romanesque Revival features in the same building.

By the beginning of the twentieth century some architects and architectural theorists were advocating a return to a more formal, scholarly approach to Gothic design, which is sometimes referred to as "Late Gothic Revival" or "Neo-Gothic."

The term "High Gothic" refers to a careful, formal approach to Gothic architecture that is inspired particularly by medieval English and French cathedrals. "Low Gothic" refers to a less formal approach to Gothic architecture, which, when it is based on medieval precedents, draws more from smaller, less ornate and more rustic parish churches.

Gothic arch (*pointed arch*)

A *Gothic arch* or *pointed arch* is an arch formed by two curved sides that come together in a point. It is one of the main distinguishing features of **Gothic** architecture. (In contrast, **Romanesque** architecture is distinguished by the use of the *round arch*.)

A pointed arch that has sides made of S-shaped curves is called an **ogee arch**. A broad Gothic arch that has sides that flatten and straighten toward the point is called a **Tudor arch**.

hexastyle (see *portico*)

Ionic (see *order*)

loggia

A *loggia* is a broad, low porch, usually only one story in height and recessed behind a row of arches (an **arcade**) or sometimes a row of columns (a **colonnade**). Some loggias are recessed into the main wall of a building or between corner towers; others project from the main wall under a flat roof or a shed roof. A loggia is very different in architectural character from a portico, which is more formal and monumental. Some Gothic Revival and Romanesque Revival churches, such as the second Crawford Street Methodist Church in Vicksburg (1899), had loggias in their front façades sheltering their entrances.

ogee; ogival

The term *ogival* is used to describe a feature, such as a window or a Moorish-style dome, in which each side has the form of an **ogee**, an S-shaped curve, and the sides are connected so as to form a point at the top. A pointed arch that has sides made of S-shaped curves is called an **ogee arch**.

order

In Classical architecture, *order* refers to any one of several traditional sets of design elements and relationships that are most easily recognized by the shapes of their distinctive columns. The various orders are sometimes described as if they were represented only by their columns, but it is important to remember that each order consists of proportions and characteristic details beyond just the design of its columns.

Ancient Greek architecture and the Greek Revival architecture that was based on it used three orders: **Doric**, **Ionic**, and **Corinthian**. Ancient Roman architecture and the Classical architecture derived from ancient Roman models used five orders: **Tuscan**, **Doric**, **Ionic**, **Corinthian**, and **Composite**. Some large, ornate buildings use more than one order, with different orders applied to separate parts of the building with a specific relationship between them. Many nineteenth- and twentieth-century buildings exhibit variations from the canonical classical orders. For example, several churches in Mississippi were designed using a variation on the Ionic order that used Greek Ionic capitals (the ornamental caps of the columns) but Roman Ionic proportions and shafts. Providing proper descriptions of the orders is beyond the scope

of this brief glossary. Readers interested in learning more about them should consult a good architecture dictionary.

peaked window

A *peaked window* is a window that has a pointed top (a **peak**) formed by two straight edges, set at an angle. The angle formed by the two sides of the peak is most commonly 90 degrees (as in windows of the old Methodist Church in Shelby), but it can also be 60 degrees (as in the windows of the old First Presbyterian Church in Pascagoula) or a shallower angle of about 120 degrees. Peaked windows are vernacular simplifications of the curved pointed windows of Gothic Revival architecture (see **Gothic arch**). They are most commonly seen on wooden Carpenter Gothic buildings built between 1850 and 1915, but they are also sometimes seen on brick buildings.

pinnacle

A *pinnacle* is a vertically positioned decorative feature that can be regarded as a miniature spire (see *spire*). Pinnacles are sometimes used, particularly in Gothic architecture, to ornament the tops of parapet walls and towers. They are commonly placed at the four corners of a church tower around the base of a spire. A pinnacle can also be used as a finial to decorate the peak of a pointed roof.

portico

In Classical architecture, a **portico** is an open porch, supported by columns, typically located on the front of a building and sheltering the main entrance. Customarily the columns support a full classical entablature above which is a triangular gable called a **pediment**. There were some Neoclassical churches built in the 1910s and 1920s, however, where the portico was purely decorative and did not shelter the entrances, which were located on either side of the portico, as was the case at the First Methodist Church of Laurel (1912–13) (where it is said to have been a later alteration), First Baptist Church of Biloxi (1924), First Baptist Church of McComb (1923–24), and First Baptist Church of Philadelphia (1927).

Traditional terminology is used to describe the shape and placement of a portico and the number of columns it contains. A portico having only two columns is called **distyle** (Greek, *distylos*, from *di-*, "two" and *stylos*, "column"). A portico containing two columns set between projecting piers or cheek walls is described as **distyle in antis** (Latin, "between antae" or "between projecting piers"). This term is also widely used to describe a two-column portico that is recessed into a wall, so that the columns are in line with the plane of the wall, but this configuration is more accurately referred to as **distyle in muris** (Latin, "within the wall"). This was a popular design for Greek Revival churches, such as the Methodist Church at Aberdeen (1859–60) and Bethel Presbyterian Church near Columbus (1844–45).

A portico that projects forward from the plane of the front wall is said to be a **prostyle** ("forward column") portico, but because porticoes are most commonly prostyle, the term is not often used, since the portico is assumed to be prostyle unless it is recessed into the wall. Prostyle porticoes are typically described by terms that indicate the number of columns—**tetrastyle** (four columns), **hexastyle** (six columns), or **octastyle** (eight columns). In formal classical architecture, it is considered awkward for a portico to have an odd number of columns, so it is very rare to see a three-column portico like those on the old First Baptist Church at Iuka (1915) and the old First Baptist Church at Ripley (1916).

The old First Baptist Church in Greenwood (circa 1907–10) and the old Temple Beth Israel in Meridian (1906) were examples of churches with projecting tetrastyle porticoes. Crystal Springs Methodist Church (1919) had a projecting hexastyle portico.

Many of the churches built in Mississippi during the 1910s and 1920s were designed with porticoes that were partially recessed—the columns themselves were placed in front of the wall plane, but the space contained within the portico was recessed behind the wall plane. In this book, and in *Historic Churches of Mississippi*, the term **semi-recessed portico** is used to describe this configuration. Examples of churches with semi-recessed porticoes include the old First Baptist Church at Amory (1918) and the old First Baptist Church at Louisville (1915).

Romanesque, Romanesque Revival

The term **Romanesque** refers to the religious architecture of Western Europe in the early medieval period, from about the ninth through the twelfth centuries.

Medieval Romanesque architecture was characterized by massive stone walls pierced by round-arched doors and windows. The interior structure of churches was typically formed from arcades of round arches and ceilings made of semicircular vaults. In the later centuries of the medieval period, Romanesque architecture was largely superseded by **Gothic** architecture (see *Gothic*).

Romanesque architecture was revived in the mid-nineteenth century as an architectural style called *Romanesque Revival* that was based on early medieval precedents. In the 1880s and 1890s a version of Romanesque Revival architecture became popular that stressed massive walls, square towers, and broad, low arches. Most notably used by the famed architect H. H. Richardson of Boston, this style is called **Richardsonian Romanesque**.

round arch

A **round arch** is an arch formed by a continuous curve in the shape of a semicircle. Round arches are used in **Romanesque** architecture, but they are also widely used in some other styles as well. (See *windows*.)

sanctuary (see **auditorium**)

spire

A *spire* is a slender, vertical structure, tapering to a point, that is placed atop a church tower or on the roof of a church, to draw attention to the fact that the building is a church. According to traditional reckoning, a spire is intended to draw the viewer's eyes heavenward. Spires are most commonly either four-sided or eight-sided, but there are also round spires and spires of more complex shapes, including a type called a **broach spire**.

A *broach spire* is a complex spire consisting of a slender octagonal upper section that rises from a broader, pyramidal lower section. The "broach" is the part of the structure that provides the transition from a square to an octagon. The purpose of the broach shape is to enable the placement of an octagonal spire on a square tower or belfry.

steeple

A *steeple* is a vertical structure on the exterior of a church, which can be located either on top of the roof or on a tower. A steeple usually contains a **belfry** (a chamber where a bell or a set of bells is hung) and is most typically topped by a *spire*; but a steeple can also be flat-topped, gabled, pyramidal-roofed, or capped by a small dome.

tetrastyle (see *portico*)

transept

A *transept* is a wing that extends to the side of a church. In traditional terminology, a transept is connected to the **nave** (the main hall where the congregation gathers) and is open to it as a continuous interior space. A wing that does not form part of the same interior space as the nave (for example, a projecting wing that contains a Sunday school classroom) is not a true transept, though it may be designed to look like a transept when viewed from the exterior.

Many medieval Gothic churches and many Gothic Revival churches were designed with a **cruciform** (cross-shaped) plan, in which the nave formed the stem of the cross, transepts to either side formed the arms, and a projecting chancel formed the top of the stem of the cross, past the arms. The old Church of Our Lady of the Gulf in Bay St. Louis (1872) had a cruciform plan.

Tudor arch (see **Gothic arch**)

Tuscan (see *order*)

vestibule

A *vestibule* is an entrance hall or lobby. In the terminology traditionally used to describe the medieval Gothic churches of England and France, an entrance lobby set within the main walls of a church is called a **narthex**. The term **vestibule** is more typically applied to a small entrance room that projects out from the main wall of the church, like an enclosed porch. Small vernacular churches in Mississippi in the nineteenth century typically did not have vestibules, which were sometimes added later, as was the case at St. Mark's Episcopal Church in Gulfport.

windows

Windows are openings in the wall of a building that allow light into the interior. They are usually filled with glass panes set into one or more frames. The frames (called sashes or casements, depending on the type) are often moveable, so that the window can be opened to allow fresh air into the building, as well as light. The placement or arrangement of windows in the design of a building is called **fenestration** (see *fenestration*).

Windows have a very wide variety of shapes, sizes, and designs. The design of the windows is an important element in the stylistic character of a building—Gothic churches will most typically have **pointed arched windows** (see *Gothic arch*). Some vernacular Gothic Revival churches have **peaked windows** (see *peaked window*). Romanesque churches will normally have **round-arched windows** (see *round arch*). Greek Revival churches usually have flat-topped rectangular windows. Churches of the Federal, Neoclassical Revival, Georgian Revival, and Federal Revival styles may have windows that are either round-arched or rectangular, or both types in the same building. The windows in the parts of a church building that contain offices and classrooms are typically rectangular regardless of the building's architectural style. There are numerous other shapes of windows besides these.

Bibliography

General Sources

The single most important source for information about specific churches and synagogues included in this book is the Historic Resources Inventory of the Historic Preservation Division of the Mississippi Department of Archives and History (MDAH). This is a continuously growing system of files about more than forty thousand historic buildings and sites in Mississippi, both surviving and nonextant, supported by a computer database. During the twenty-one years that I worked as chief architectural historian for MDAH, I organized this system of files, and I used it and added to it on an almost daily basis.

The **Sanborn fire insurance maps** are another extremely helpful source for numerous cities and towns in Mississippi. These maps, issued for many communities at roughly five-year intervals from the 1880s or 1890s through the 1920s, with some later updates, show the locations and "footprints" of every building that was standing in the area covered by the maps at the time each map was made. There is a collection of Sanborn maps for Mississippi on microfilm at the MDAH Library. MDAH also has some original Sanborn maps, for which access is very limited. The most convenient way to use the Sanborn maps is through an Internet Web site, but it is only available though subscription.

City directories were another important source, particularly for churches in Jackson. There is an extensive collection of Jackson city directories available in the open reference area of the Eudora Welty Library in Jackson.

The *Inventory of the Church Records, 1936–1941* (MDAH Archives Series 450) is a very large but very miscellaneous assemblage of information on churches in Mississippi, arranged by county in file folders, compiled under the auspices of the Works Progress Administration from 1936 to 1941. The records pertain mostly to the organizational history of the churches, but there is also some scattered architectural information.

In some cases, useful information about lost churches in Mississippi was found on the Internet, most typically on the Web sites maintained by individual churches. I was very disappointed to see that many active churches do not have Web sites, and many that do have Web sites do not include information about the history of the congregation. It would be good for every active religious congregation to have its own Web site, and for every Web site to include a history of the church!

The most important source for the photographs used in this book was the vast collection of photographs at the library of the Mississippi Department of Archives and History. That collection is made up of numerous smaller component collections. Of those, the most important was the Forrest L. Cooper Postcard Collection (which consists of over four thousand postcards).

Some of the images used in the book are from postcards obtained by purchase from numerous dealers. The most useful and accessible source of historic postcards is the network of postcard dealers on eBay.

Published Works with Specific Information about Churches in Mississippi

Most of these works can be found at the library of the Mississippi Department of Archives and History.

Alcorn County Historical Association. *The History of Alcorn County*. Dallas, Tex.: National Share Graphics, Inc., 1983.

This thick volume of information about the history and families of Alcorn County includes historical information about many churches, including First Baptist Church of Corinth, First Methodist Church of Corinth, and First Presbyterian Church of Corinth.

Art Work of Mississippi. Chicago: Gravure Illustration Company, 1901.

This rare publication (copies of which are in the collection of the MDAH Library) has a misleading name. It is actually a collection of photographs of some major architectural works in Mississippi as they appeared about 1900, including First Baptist Church in Jackson, First Baptist Church in Meridian, and First Presbyterian Church in Yazoo City.

Bass, Jimmy (photographs) and Nell Davis (text). *A Pictorial History of Laurel, Mississippi*. Laurel, Miss.: privately published, 1991.

This book includes historical information about churches in Laurel, including First Baptist Church, First Methodist Church, and First Presbyterian Church.

Black, John T. *Faith of Our Fathers: How Religion Has Influenced the History of Greenville, Mississippi*. Greenville, Miss., 2005.

This book contains historical information about churches in Greenville.

Brinson, Carroll. *Jackson, a Special Kind of Place*. Jackson, Miss.: City of Jackson, 1976.

A pictorial history of Jackson that contains some information about the older churches.

The Buildings of Biloxi: An Architectural Survey. Biloxi: City of Biloxi, 1976, revised and reissued in 2000.

A detailed architectural survey of historic buildings in Biloxi, Mississippi.

Cain, J. B. *Magnolia Methodist Church, 1856–1956*. Nashville: Parthenon Press, 1961.

This is a history of Magnolia Methodist Church in Magnolia, Mississippi.

Cotton, Gordon A. *Vicksburg (Images of America)*. Charleston, S.C.: Arcadia Publishing, 1999.

A collection of old photographs of Vicksburg, that contains some information about older churches.

———. *Vicksburg: Town and Country (Images of America)*. Charleston, S.C.: Arcadia Publishing, 2001.

Another collection of old photographs of Vicksburg that contains some information about older churches.

Crigler, T. W., ed. *History of the First Baptist Church, 1835–1960, Macon, Mississippi*. Macon: First Baptist Church, 1960.

A history of First Baptist Church in Macon, Mississippi.

Crocker, Mary Wallace. *Historic Architecture in Mississippi*. Jackson: University Press of Mississippi, 1973.

This pioneering but now very dated book is a broad architectural survey of notable historic buildings in Mississippi.

Douglas, Ed Polk. *Architecture in Claiborne County, Mississippi: A Selective Guide*. Jackson: Mississippi Department of Archives and History, 1974.

A detailed architectural survey of historic buildings in Port Gibson and rural Claiborne County, Mississippi.

The Episcopal Church in Mississippi, 1763–1992. Jackson: The Episcopal Diocese of Mississippi, 1992.

A history of the Episcopal Diocese of Mississippi, containing information about all the Episcopal churches of the state, past and present. It is particularly informative in regard to St. Columb's Chapel in Jackson.

Everman, Grace G., and Lavinia D. Fort, eds. *History of St. James Church, Greenville, Mississippi, 1869–1946*. Greenville, Miss.: St. James Episcopal Church, 1946.

A history of St. James Episcopal Church, Greenville, Mississippi.

Grimsley, Reagan L. *Hattiesburg in Vintage Postcards*. Charleston, S.C.: Arcadia Publishing, 2004.

A collection of old postcard images of Hattiesburg, which contains some information about older churches.

Hattiesburg Area Historical Society. *History of Forrest County.* Hattiesburg: Hattiesburg Area Historical Society, 2000.

A compendium of historical information about Hattiesburg and Forrest County.

Historic Vicksburg Walking Tour Guide. Vicksburg: Vicksburg Foundation for Historic Preservation, 1987.

This interesting and informative booklet contains information about existing historic buildings in Vicksburg along with old photographs of nonextant buildings, such as the old Crawford Street Methodist Church of 1899.

The Hundredth Anniversary of the First Baptist Church—The Highlights of One Hundred Years (typescript booklet). Corinth, Miss.: First Baptist Church, 1955.

A short history of First Baptist Church in Corinth, Mississippi.

Jackson Chamber of Commerce. *The Book of Jackson.* Jackson, Miss.: Jackson Chamber of Commerce, 1928.

This is a promotional booklet that was produced by the Jackson Chamber of Commerce. It includes photographs of many of the churches that were active in Jackson in 1928. It was the source of the photographs of the First Church of Christ, Scientist and the Seventh Day Adventist Church that are used in Lost Churches of Mississippi.

Jenkins, William L. *Mississippi United Methodist Churches: Two Hundred Years of Heritage and Hope.* Franklin, Tenn.: Providence House, 1998.

This is an encyclopedic compilation of historical information about every United Methodist church in Mississippi that was active about 1998. Unfortunately, the amount and quality of the information varies considerably from church to church. For some there is a very extensive history, but for others there is nothing more than a mailing address, and there is no information about extinct congregations.

Jones, William Burwell. *Methodism in the Mississippi Conference, 1870–1894.* Jackson: Mississippi Conference Historical Society, 1951.

A chronological history of the Mississippi Methodist Conference from 1870 to 1894, compiled from minutes and reports of its annual meetings.

Julien, Carl (photographs) and Daniel W. Hollis (text). *Look to the Rock: One Hundred Ante-bellum Presbyterian Churches of the South.* Richmond: John Knox Press, 1961.

This book includes several antebellum churches in Mississippi—First Presbyterian Church in Holly Springs, Rodney Presbyterian Church in Rodney, Carmel Presbyterian Church near Natchez, College Presbyterian Church at College Hill near Oxford, and Bethel Presbyterian Church near Columbus. Of these, only Bethel no longer stands.

Kimbrough, Julie L. *Jackson (Images of America).* Charleston, S.C.: Arcadia Publishing, 1998.

A collection of old photographs of Jackson, which contains some information about older churches.

Lane, Mills. *Architecture of the Old South: Mississippi and Alabama.* New York: Abbeville Press, 1989.

A selective overview of the antebellum architecture of Mississippi and Alabama, including several notable churches.

Lann, Felix, and Carolyn Evans Sauter. *Methodism in Aberdeen: A Scrapbook of Historical Sketches from 1836 to 1957.* Aberdeen, Miss.: First United Methodist Church, 1986.

A history of First Methodist Church in Aberdeen, Mississippi.

Lindsey, J. Allen. *Methodism in the Mississippi Conference, 1894–1919.* Jackson: Mississippi Conference Historical Society, 1964.

A chronological history of the Mississippi Methodist Conference from 1894 to 1919, compiled from minutes and reports of its annual meetings.

Lipscomb, W. L. *A History of Columbus, Mississippi, During the 19th Century.* Birmingham, Ala.: Press of Dispatch Printing Company, 1909.

This book contains information about early churches in Columbus, Mississippi. Of particular interest is the account of the building of First Baptist Church, 1838–40.

Lobb, Craig J. *History of the First Christian Church of Jackson, Mississippi.* Jackson, Miss.: First Christian Church, 1987.

A history of First Christian Church in Jackson, Mississippi.

McCain, William D. *The Story of Jackson: A History of the Capital of Mississippi, 1821–1951.* Vol. 1. Jackson, Miss.: J. F. Hyer Pub. Co., 1953.

This is a superb source of extensive, well-documented historical information about churches in Jackson, especially the older downtown churches.

McLemore, Richard Aubry, and Namie Pitts McLemore. *The History of First Baptist Church of Jackson, Mississippi.* Jackson: Hederman Brothers, 1976.

A history of First Baptist Church in Jackson, Mississippi.

Miller, Mary Carol. *Lost Landmarks of Mississippi.* Jackson: University Press of Mississippi, 2002.

This book, which was one of the inspirations for Lost Churches of Mississippi, *addresses a wide range of "lost" buildings and other properties. It contains information about twelve nonextant churches and synagogues. Five are buildings that are also included in* Lost Churches of Mississippi: *the old First Baptist Church of Columbus, old St. Paul's Catholic Church in Vicksburg, old Temple Beth Israel in Jackson, the second Church of the Redeemer in Biloxi, and the old First Baptist Church of Greenwood. Seven others are not included in* Lost Churches of Mississippi: *St. John's Episcopal Church at Glen Allan in Washington County, the Cumberland Presbyterian Church at Oxford, the old First Christian Church of Columbus, old Temple Anshe Chesed in Vicksburg, old Temple B'nai Israel in Natchez, Temple Beth Israel in Woodville, and the old First Baptist Church of Ripley.*

Mississippi Historical Records Survey. *Inventory of the Church and Synagogue Archives of Mississippi: Jewish Congregations and Organizations.* Jackson, Miss.: Mississippi State Conference, B'nai B'rith, 1940.

This is a printed, bound volume of information about the history of every Jewish congregation and organization in Mississippi, including dissolved congregations, arranged chronologically by the age of the congregation, compiled under the auspices of the Works Progress Administration.

Mississippi Historical Records Survey. *Inventory of the Church Archives of Mississippi—Protestant Episcopal Church—Diocese of Mississippi.* Jackson, Miss.: Mississippi Historical Records Survey Project, 1940.

This is a printed, bound volume of information about the history of every Episcopal congregation in Mississippi, including dissolved congregations and missions, arranged chronologically by the age of the congregation, compiled under the auspices of the Works Progress Administration.

Monroe County Book Committee. *A History of Monroe County, Mississippi.* Dallas, Tex.: Curtis Media, 1988.

This thick volume of information about the history and families of Monroe County includes historical information about numerous churches, including the First Baptist Church of Aberdeen, the First Methodist Church of Aberdeen, the First Baptist Church of Amory, and the First Methodist Church of Amory.

Moulder, Bob V. (photographs) and Carl McIntyre (text). *Shrines to Tomorrow.* Jackson: privately published, 1971.

This interesting softcover book, now long out of print and hard to find, consists of photographs and brief historical notes about numerous churches that were standing in Mississippi around 1968–70, some of which have since been lost. Among the churches that are now lost that were included in this book are the second Church of the Redeemer in Biloxi, First Baptist Church in Biloxi, First Baptist Church in Greenwood, St. Mark's Episcopal Church in Gulfport, Trinity Episcopal Church in Pass Christian, First Baptist Church in West Point, and the Presbyterian Church in West Point. Some of the photographs from this book are now in the photographic collections of the MDAH Library.

Pace, Sherry (photographs) and Richard J. Cawthon (text). *Historic Churches of Mississippi.* Jackson: University Press of Mississippi, 2007.

This is a collection of color photographs of historic churches in Mississippi. It also contains an introductory essay which provides a concise history of the religious architecture of Mississippi from the 1820s to the 1920s.

Smith, Mary Lorraine, ed. *Historic Churches of the South.* Atlanta: Tupper & Love, Inc. 1952.

A miscellaneous collection of short articles about a variety of historic churches throughout the South, including the second Church of the Redeemer in Biloxi.

Taylor, S. W. *Mississippi: The Magnolia State—A Short Concise History.* New Orleans: Horace M. Goddard and Company, 1904–1905.

This brief book includes numerous photos of buildings, mostly in Jackson and Greenville, as of about 1904.

Turitz, Leo, and Evelyn Turitz. *Jews in Early Mississippi.* Jackson, Miss.: University Press of Mississippi, 1983.

Provides information about several of the state's early Jewish synagogues.

Weaver, Mary Warriner. *And Are We Yet Alive? The Story of the Beginning and Progress of the Methodist Church in Corinth, Mississippi, 1799–1953.* Corinth, Miss.: First Methodist Church, 1955.

A short history of First Methodist Church in Corinth, Mississippi.

Welch, Elizabeth Claire. "Ecclesiology: Its Influence on the Gothic Revival Episcopal Church in Antebellum Mississippi." Master's thesis, School of Architecture, University of Virginia, January 1981.

A study of antebellum Gothic Revival religious architecture in Mississippi.

Whittington, Will M. *Early History and Progress of First Baptist Church of Greenwood.* Greenwood, Miss.: First Baptist Church, 1965.

This is a history of First Baptist Church in Greenwood, Mississippi.

Winter, R. Milton. *Thy Dwellings Fair: Churches of Saint Andrew Presbytery.* Oxford, Miss.: The Presbytery of Saint Andrew, 2000.

This is a compilation of information about the churches affiliated with the Presbyterian Church, USA, in Saint Andrew Presbytery, which is roughly the northern half of Mississippi. It contains photos of all the churches that were members of the presbytery in about 2000, but it has very little historical information about them.

Womack, Tom. *A History of the First Baptist Church of West Point, Mississippi, 1885–1985.* West Point, Miss.: Sullivan's Printing Company, 1987.

A history of First Baptist Church in West Point, Mississippi.

Yalobusha Historical Society, Heritage Committee. *Yalobusha County History.* Dallas, Tex.: National Share Graphics, Inc., 1982.

This thick volume of information about the history and families of Yalobusha County includes historical information about numerous churches, including the Church of the Nativity in Water Valley, the First Baptist Church of Water Valley, and Water Valley Methodist Church.

Yazoo Historical Association. *Yazoo County Story.* Fort Worth, Tex.: University Supply & Equipment Co., 1958.

A collection of miscellaneous information about the history of Yazoo County, with numerous photographs.

Published Works with Information about the History of Religious Architecture in the United States

There is no single book that provides a satisfactory history or survey of religious architecture in the South. There are several books that present a broad overview of the history of religious architecture in the United States, but these are typically so broad as to be of little use in understanding the context of Mississippi's religious architecture. To my knowledge, the only published overview of the history of church architecture in Mississippi is "Religious Architecture in Mississippi from the 1820s through the 1920s," the introductory essay I wrote for *Historic Churches of Mississippi.* Most books and articles that directly examine religious architecture in the South are limited to the Greek Revival or the Gothic Revival architecture of the antebellum period. There is apparently no broad overview that examines late Victorian and early twentieth-century religious architecture in the southern states. There are a few books that present a coherent overview of the history of religious architecture in a single state. One of the best of these is:

Robinson, Willard B. *Reflections of Faith: Houses of Worship in the Lone Star State.* Waco, Tex.: Baylor University Press, 1994.

A history of religious architecture in Texas.

Some other books that provide information about either the broader context of American religious architecture or the religious architecture of Mississippi and the South are:

Howe, Jeffery. *Houses of Worship: An Identification Guide to the History and Styles of American Religious Architecture.* San Diego, Cal.: Thunder Bay Press, 2003.

An extremely broad overview of American religious architecture that focuses almost entirely on the urban Northeast and the Upper Midwest, with almost nothing about the South.

Kidder, F. E. *Churches and Chapels.* New York: William T. Comstock, 1900.

An architectural treatise about building churches, written by architect Franklin E. Kidder (1859–1905) of Denver,

Colorado. *The book includes pictures of some churches designed by Kidder and other architects, including a design that incorporates a tower very similar to those on the old First Methodist Church in Clarksdale and the old Methodist Church in Edwards.*

Kilde, Jeanne Halgren. *When Church Became Theatre: The Transformation of Evangelical Architecture and Worship in Nineteenth-Century America.* New York: Oxford University Press, 2005 (© 2002).

A thoughtful, well-written, and very informative examination of the origins and development of the "auditorium church" in the late nineteenth century, along with some discussion of its decline and eventual resurgence in popularity in the twentieth century, but it is focused almost entirely on the urban Northeast and the Upper Midwest and says nothing about the auditorium-plan churches of the South.

Lane, Mills. *Architecture of the Old South* (summary volume). New York: Abbeville Publishers (A Beehive Press Book), 1993.

A broad overview of the architecture of the South from the Colonial period to the Civil War. It concentrates primarily on secular architecture, but does include some churches.

Patrick, James. "Ecclesiological Gothic in the Antebellum South." *Winterthur Portfolio* 15:2 (September 1980).

An article about Gothic architecture in the south from about the 1840s to 1860. It bridges the national perspective of Phoebe Stanton's The Gothic Revival & American Church Architecture *and the Mississippi perspective of Elizabeth Claire Welch's "Ecclesiology: Its Influence on the Gothic Revival Episcopal Church in Antebellum Mississippi."*

Price, Benjamin D., and Max Charles Price. *Church Plans.* Atlantic Highlands, N. J.: privately published, 1906.

This was the thirty-first annual catalog of church plans that were available by mail order from Benjamin D. Price. Many churches in Mississippi were built from mail-order plans shown in this book.

Stanton, Phoebe. *The Gothic Revival & American Church Architecture: An Episode in Taste, 1840–1856.* Baltimore: The Johns Hopkins Press, 1968.

A detailed history of the origins of Gothic Revival religious architecture in the United States.

Some Other Published Works Used as Sources

Lay, K. Edward. *The Architecture of Jefferson Country.* Charlottesville: University Press of Virginia, 2000.

A study of the architecture of Albemarle County, Virginia (home of Thomas Jefferson and the University of Virginia), this book provides an explanation of the term "distyle in muris," which architectural historians in Virginia use in preference to the less accurate term "distyle in antis" to describe the porch configuration seen on churches such as the old Methodist Church in Aberdeen and Bethel Presbyterian Church near Columbus.

Peatross, C. Ford, and Robert O. Mellown. *William Nichols, Architect.* Exhibit catalog. Tuscaloosa: University of Alabama Art Gallery, 1979.

This booklet summarizes the life and work of the architect of Mississippi's Old Capitol, who also designed several churches, including the original First Presbyterian Church in Jackson.

Illustration Credits

Frontis Crawford Street Methodist Church (II) (1899). Photograph courtesy of the Old Courthouse Museum, Vicksburg.

p. 7 First Methodist Church, Aberdeen (1859–60). A pencil drawing by the author, based on an old photograph.

p. 8 First Baptist Church, Aberdeen (1891–94). From a postcard in the Forrest Lamar Cooper Postcard Collection (PI/1992.0001, no. 3699), courtesy of the Mississippi Department of Archives and History.

p. 10 First Methodist Church, Amory (1914). From a postcard in the Forrest Lamar Cooper Postcard Collection (PI/1992.0001, no. 1786), courtesy of the Mississippi Department of Archives and History.

p. 11 First Methodist Church, Amory. Drawing of site plan by Pete Halverson, based on a sketch by the author.

p. 12 First Baptist Church, Amory (1918). From a postcard in the Postcard Negative Collection (PI/1985.0031, no. 3), courtesy of the Mississippi Department of Archives and History.

p. 13 Church of Our Lady of the Gulf (Catholic), Bay St. Louis (1872). From a postcard in a private collection.

p. 14 First Baptist Church, Belzoni (1922). From a postcard in the Belzoni Photograph Collection (PI/CI/1982.0129, no. 14), courtesy of the Mississippi Department of Archives and History.

p. 15 Church of the Redeemer (I), Biloxi (1873–74). From a postcard in the Forrest Lamar Cooper Postcard Collection (PI/1992.0001, no. 421), courtesy of the Mississippi Department of Archives and History.

p. 16 Church of the Redeemer (II), Biloxi (1891). From a postcard (PI/1984.0012, no. 5), courtesy of the Mississippi Department of Archives and History.

p. 17 Interior of the Church of the Redeemer (II), Biloxi. From a postcard in the collection of the author.

p. 18 Tower of the Church of the Redeemer (II), Biloxi. Photograph courtesy of the Historic Preservation Division, Mississippi Department of Archives and History.

p. 19 Main Street Methodist Church, Biloxi (1904–5). From a postcard in the Forrest Lamar Cooper Postcard Collection (PI/1992.0001, no. 619), courtesy of the Mississippi Department of Archives and History.

p. 20 First Baptist Church, Biloxi (1924). From a postcard (PI/1985.0041, no. 140), courtesy of the Mississippi Department of Archives and History.

p. 22 First Methodist Church, Booneville (1897, 1901). From a postcard in the Forrest Lamar Cooper Postcard Collection (PI/1992.0001, no. 4418), courtesy of the Mississippi Department of Archives and History.

p. 23 Perspective No. 220. From Benjamin D. Price and Max Charles Price, *Church Plans* (1906).

p. 24 Brandon Methodist Church, Brandon (1867–73). WPA photograph (PI/SF/CH/ 1986.0033, no. 33), courtesy of the Mississippi Department of Archives and History.

p. 26 First Methodist Church, Brookhaven (1904). From a postcard in the Forrest Lamar Cooper Postcard Collection (PI/1992.0001, no. 1950), courtesy of the Mississippi Department of Archives and History.

p. 27 Perspective No. 169. From Benjamin D. Price and Max Charles Price, *Church Plans* (1906), in the collection of the author.

p. 27 First Methodist Church, Hinton, West Virginia. From a postcard in the collection of the author.

p. 27 Methodist Church, Kinsley, Kansas. From a postcard in the collection of the author.

p. 29 Cover of Benjamin D. Price and Max Charles Price, *Church Plans* (1906), in the collection of the author.

p. 30 Presbyterian Church (later Baptist Church), Buena Vista (1860). WPA photograph (Official Records Series 1631, no. 132), courtesy of the Mississippi Department of Archives and History.

p. 32 Presbyterian Church, Canton (1852–53). Photograph (PI/CI/1983.0028, no. 29), courtesy of the Mississippi Department of Archives and History.

p. 34 Temple B'nai Israel, Canton (1877). Photograph (PI/CI/1983.0028, no. 2), courtesy of the Mississippi Department of Archives and History.

p. 35 First Methodist Church, Clarksdale (1897). From a postcard in the Forrest Lamar Cooper Postcard Collection (PI/1992.0001, no. 3496), courtesy of the Mississippi Department of Archives and History.

p. 36 First Baptist Church, Dade City, Florida. Photograph courtesy of the State Archives of Florida.

p. 37 Illustration from F. E. Kidder, *Churches and Chapels* (1900).

p. 38 First Presbyterian Church, Clarksdale (circa 1915–17). From a postcard in the collection of the author.

p. 39 First Christian Church, Clarksdale (1923–29). Photograph courtesy of the Historic Preservation Division, Mississippi Department of Archives and History.

p. 41 Baptist Church, Collins (1925). WPA photograph (Official Records Series 1631, no. 320), courtesy of the Mississippi Department of Archives and History.

p. 42 First Baptist Church, Columbia (1911–12). From a postcard in the Postcard Negative Collection (PI/1985.0031, no. 217), courtesy of the Mississippi Department of Archives and History.

p. 44 First Baptist Church, Columbus. From a postcard in the Forrest Lamar Cooper Postcard Collection (PI/1992.0001, no. 3816), courtesy of the Mississippi Department of Archives and History.

p. 45 First Baptist Church (I), Columbus (1838–40). From a photograph in *Art Work of Mississippi* (1901), courtesy of the Mississippi Department of Archives and History.

p. 46 The Lyceum, University of Mississippi. Photograph courtesy of Special Collections, University of Mississippi Libraries.

p. 48 Bethel Presbyterian Church, south of Columbus (1844–45). Photograph courtesy of the Historic Preservation Division, Mississippi Department of Archives and History.

p. 49 Robinson Springs Methodist Church, Elmore County, Alabama. Photograph from the Historic American Buildings Survey, Library of Congress, Washington, D.C.

p. 49 Ruins of Bethel Presbyterian Church after the tornado of November 10, 2002. Photograph courtesy of the Historic Preservation Division, Mississippi Department of Archives and History.

p. 50 First Methodist Church, Corinth (1890–92). From a postcard in the collection of the author.

p. 51 First Methodist Church, Corinth, in the 1930s. WPA photograph (Official Records Series 1631, no. 90), courtesy of the Mississippi Department of Archives and History.

p. 52 First Baptist Church, Corinth (1894–95). From a postcard in the Forrest Lamar Cooper Postcard Collection (PI/1992.0001, no. 4350), courtesy of the Mississippi Department of Archives and History.

p. 53 First Baptist Church, Corinth, in the 1930s. WPA photograph (Official Records Series 1631, no. 89), courtesy of the Mississippi Department of Archives and History.

p. 53 Remnants of old First Baptist Church, Corinth, in 2008. Photograph courtesy of Mrs. Diana Sanders of Corinth.

p. 55 First Presbyterian Church, Corinth (1894–96). WPA photograph (Official Records Series 1631, no. 91), courtesy of the Mississippi Department of Archives and History.

p. 56 Perspective No. 220. From Benjamin D. Price and Max Charles Price, *Church Plans* (1906).

p. 57 First Presbyterian Church, Corinth (1894–96). From a postcard in the collection of the author.

p. 57 First Presbyterian Church, Berwick, Pennsylvania. From a postcard in the collection of the author.

p. 58 Crystal Springs Methodist Church, Crystal Springs (1919). Photograph courtesy of the Historic Preservation Division, Mississippi Department of Archives and History.

p. 58 Dresden Methodist Church, Dresden, Tennessee. From a postcard in the collection of the author.

p. 60 Drew Baptist Church, Drew (1920). WPA photograph (Official Records Series 1631, no. 89), courtesy of the Mississippi Department of Archives and History.

p. 61 First Baptist Church, Durant (1898). From a postcard in the Forrest Lamar Cooper Postcard Collection (PI/1992.0001, no. 4272), courtesy of the Mississippi Department of Archives and History.

p. 62 Edwards Methodist Church, Edwards (1899). From a postcard in the Forrest Lamar Cooper Postcard Collection (PI/1992.0001, no. 2698), courtesy of the Mississippi Department of Archives and History.

p. 63 St. James Episcopal Church, Greenville (1885–86 and later). Photograph in the Greenville Photographs Collection (PI/CI/G74.4, no. 79), courtesy of the Mississippi Department of Archives and History.

p. 64 St. James, Port Gibson. From Ed Polk Douglas, *Architecture in Claiborne County, Mississippi: A Selective Guide* (Jackson: Mississippi Department of Archives and History, 1974), courtesy of the Mississippi Department of Archives and History.

p. 65 First Presbyterian Church, Greenville (1901–2). WPA photograph courtesy of the Historic Preservation Division, Mississippi Department of Archives and History.

p. 66 First Methodist Church, Greenville (1903–4). Photograph in the Greenville Photographs Collection (PI/CI/G74.4, no. 79), courtesy of the Mississippi Department of Archives and History.

p. 67 First Methodist Church, Greenville, in 1930s. WPA photograph courtesy of the Historic Preservation Division, Mississippi Department of Archives and History.

p. 67 Methodist Church, Front Royal, Virginia. From a postcard in the collection of the author.

p. 70 First Baptist Church, Greenville (1906–7). From a postcard in the Forrest Lamar Cooper Postcard Collection (PI/1992.0001, no. 3288), courtesy of the Mississippi Department of Archives and History.

p. 71 First Baptist Church, Greenville, architectural drawing. From a postcard in the Forrest Lamar Cooper Postcard Collection (PI/1992.0001, no. 3321), courtesy of the Mississippi Department of Archives and History.

p. 71 Pleasant Ridge Methodist Church, Cincinnati, Ohio. From a postcard, courtesy of the Collection of the Public Library of Cincinnati and Hamilton County.

p. 72 First Baptist Church, Greenwood (1907–10). WPA photograph (PI/SF/CH/ 1986.0033, no. 3), courtesy of the Mississippi Department of Archives and History.

p. 73 First Baptist Church, Shreveport, Louisiana. From a postcard in the collection of the author.

p. 73 St. Luke's Methodist Church, Oklahoma City, Oklahoma. From a postcard in the collection of the author.

p. 74 First Baptist Church, Chickasha, Oklahoma. From a postcard in the collection of the author.

p. 74 Beech Street Baptist Church, Texarkana, Arkansas. From a postcard in the collection of the author.

p. 77 First Baptist Church, Grenada (1888). From a postcard in the Forrest Lamar Cooper Postcard Collection (PI/1992.0001, no. 3397), courtesy of the Mississippi Department of Archives and History.

p. 78 Old First Baptist Church, Ithaca, Michigan. From a postcard in the collection of the author.

p. 78 Old First Baptist Church, Geneseo, New York. From a postcard in the collection of the author.

p. 78 First Baptist Church, Grenada, in 1930s. WPA photograph (PI/SF/CH/ 1986.0033, no. 5), courtesy of the Mississippi Department of Archives and History.

p. 79 St. Mark's Episcopal Church, Gulfport (Mississippi City) (1855). Photograph courtesy of the Historic Preservation Division, Mississippi Department of Archives and History.

p. 80 St. Mark's Episcopal Church, Gulfport, in 1986. Photograph by the author.

p. 81 First Baptist Church, Gulfport (1915). From a postcard in the collection of the author.

p. 82 First Baptist Church, Gulfport, in 1950. From a postcard in the collection of the author.

p. 83 St. John the Evangelist Catholic Church, Gulfport (1922-24). From a postcard in the collection of the author.

p. 85 Main Street Presbyterian Church, Hattiesburg (1887, 1900). From a postcard in the Forrest Lamar Cooper Postcard Collection (PI/1992.0001, no. 1384), courtesy of the Mississippi Department of Archives and History.

p. 86 Sacred Heart Catholic Church, Hattiesburg (1900). One of the eight churches in Hattiesburg shown on an old postcard in the Forrest Lamar Cooper Postcard Collection (PI/1992.0001, no. 1372), courtesy of the Mississippi Department of Archives and History.

p. 88 First Baptist Church, Hattiesburg (1900–1). From a postcard in the Forrest Lamar Cooper Postcard Collection (PI/1992.0001, no. 1398), courtesy of the Mississippi Department of Archives and History.

p. 89 First Baptist Church, Hattiesburg. Photograph courtesy of the Hattiesburg Area Historical Society.

p. 89 Old sanctuary, First Baptist Church, Elberton, Georgia. Photograph by James D. Cawthon, in the collection of the author.

p. 89 Central Methodist Church in Albany (later part of Decatur), Alabama. From a postcard in the collection of the author.

p. 90 Hazlehurst Baptist Church, Hazlehurst (1892–93). From a postcard in the collection of the author.

p. 91 First Baptist Church, Iuka (1915). WPA photograph, courtesy of the Mississippi Department of Archives and History.

p. 92 Methodist Church (I), Jackson (1838–39). Photograph by E. von Seutter (PI/CH/M43.5, no. 1), courtesy of the Mississippi Department of Archives and History.

p. 92 Christ Church, Tuscaloosa, Alabama. Old photograph from the Historic American Buildings Survey, Library of Congress, Washington, D.C.

p. 94 First Presbyterian Church (I), Jackson (1843–46, 1852). Part of a panoramic photograph of Jackson made by E. von Seutter, courtesy of the Mississippi Department of Archives and History.

p. 95 First Presbyterian Church (I), Jackson. Photograph courtesy of the Mississippi Department of Archives and History.

p. 96 First Christian Church (I), Jackson (circa 1845–50). From a stereo photograph by E. von Seutter

(PI/1985.0032, no. 3), courtesy of the Mississippi Department of Archives and History.

p. 97 St. Peter's Catholic Church (later Holy Ghost Catholic Church), Jackson (1867–69). Photograph courtesy of the Roman Catholic Diocese of Jackson Archives.

p. 98 Holy Ghost Catholic Church, Jackson. Photograph courtesy of the Roman Catholic Diocese of Jackson Archives.

p. 99 St. Andrew's Episcopal Church (II), Jackson (1869–73). From a stereo photograph by E. von Seutter (PI/1985.0032, no. 14), courtesy of the Mississippi Department of Archives and History.

p. 101 Temple Beth Israel (II), Jackson (1874–75). From a stereo photograph by E. von Seutter (PI/1985.0032, no. 13), courtesy of the Mississippi Department of Archives and History.

p. 102 Temple Beth Israel (II), Jackson, in the late 1930s. WPA photograph courtesy of the Historic Preservation Division, Mississippi Department of Archives and History.

p. 104 First Methodist Church (II), Jackson (1883). Photograph made by Albert E. Daniel in 1907 (PI/Z/970, no. 11), in the Albert E. Daniel Collection at the MDAH Library, courtesy of the Mississippi Department of Archives and History.

p. 106 St. Columb's Chapel, Jackson (1892). From a postcard in the collection of the author. There is also a copy of this postcard (PI/1991.0016, no. 11) in the Mosby Postcard Collection of the Mississippi Department of Archives and History.

p. 108 First Presbyterian Church (II), Jackson (1892–93). Photograph courtesy of the Historic Preservation Division, Mississippi Department of Archives and History.

p. 109 First Presbyterian Church (II), Jackson, being demolished. Photograph (PI/COL/1984.0019, no. 14) from the Lars Johnson Collection, courtesy of the Mississippi Department of Archives and History.

p. 110 First Christian Church (III), Jackson (1893), tower. Photograph courtesy of the Historic Preservation Division, Mississippi Department of Archives and History.

p. 111 Advertisement from *The Messenger* (1894). Courtesy of the Historic Preservation Division, Mississippi Department of Archives and History.

p. 111 First Christian Church (III), Jackson, in the 1930s, side view. WPA photograph, courtesy of the Historic Preservation Division, Mississippi Department of Archives and History.

p. 112 First Baptist Church, Jackson (1891–1900). From a photograph in *Art Work of Mississippi* (1901), courtesy of the Mississippi Department of Archives and History.

p. 113 First Baptist Church, Colorado Springs, Colorado. From a postcard in the collection of the author.

p. 114 Griffith Memorial Baptist Church, Jackson (1907). Photograph (from PI/WPA/SF/churches), courtesy of the Mississippi Department of Archives and History.

p. 116 First Church of Christ, Scientist, Jackson (1911). From a photograph in *The Book of Jackson* (1928), courtesy of the Mississippi Department of Archives and History.

p. 117 Seventh Day Adventist Church, Jackson (circa 1915). From a photograph in *The Book of Jackson* (1928), courtesy of the Mississippi Department of Archives and History. Visible to the right of the name of the church in this image are three pinnacles of a church tower from another photograph on the same page of *The Book of Jackson*.

p. 118 Temple Beth Israel (III), Jackson (circa 1940). Photograph courtesy of the Mississippi Department of Archives and History.

p. 119 First Presbyterian Church, Laurel (1901–2). From a postcard in the Forrest Lamar Cooper Postcard Collection (PI/1992.0001, no. 1878), courtesy of the Mississippi Department of Archives and History.

p. 120 First Methodist Church, Laurel (1912–13). From a postcard in the Postcard Negative Collection (PI/1985.0031, no. 578), courtesy of the Mississippi Department of Archives and History.

p. 121 First Baptist Church, Laurel (1920). From a postcard in the collection of the author.

p. 122 All Saints Episcopal Church, Long Beach (1895). From a postcard in the Forrest Lamar Cooper Postcard Collection (PI/1992.0001, no. 236), courtesy of the Mississippi Department of Archives and History.

p. 124 Louisville Presbyterian Church, Louisville (circa 1890). One of five churches pictured on a postcard (PI/1992.0001, no. 3593) in the Forrest Lamar Cooper Postcard Collection, courtesy of the Mississippi Department of Archives and History.

p. 125 Perspective No. 19A. From Benjamin D. Price and Max Charles Price, *Church Plans* (1906), in the collection of the author.

p. 125 Grace Linn Methodist Church, Hartland, Maine. From a postcard in the collection of the author.

p. 126 First Baptist Church, Louisville (1915). WPA photograph, courtesy of the Mississippi Department of Archives and History.

p. 127 First Baptist Church, Louisville. Drawing of site plan by Pete Halverson, based on a sketch by the author.

p. 128 First Baptist Church, Macon (1852). Courtesy of the Historic Preservation Division, Mississippi Department of Archives and History.

p. 130 Macon Presbyterian Church, Macon (1890). From a postcard in the Forrest Lamar Cooper Postcard Collection (PI/1992.0001, no. 3562), courtesy of the Mississippi Department of Archives and History.

p. 132 First Baptist Church, Magnolia (1895). From a postcard in the Forrest Lamar Cooper Postcard Collection (PI/1992.0001, no. 2557), courtesy of the Mississippi Department of Archives and History.

p. 133 Magnolia Methodist Church, Magnolia (1898). From a postcard in the Forrest Lamar Cooper Postcard Collection (PI/1992.0001, no. 2555), courtesy of the Mississippi Department of Archives and History.

p. 134 St. Alphonsus Catholic Church, McComb (1875–76). From a postcard in the Forrest Lamar Cooper Postcard Collection (PI/1992.0001, no. 47), courtesy of the Mississippi Department of Archives and History.

p. 135 First Baptist Church (III), McComb (1905). From a postcard in the Forrest Lamar Cooper Postcard Collection (PI/1992.0001, no. 33), courtesy of the Mississippi Department of Archives and History.

p. 136 Centenary Methodist Church, McComb (1906). From a postcard in the Forrest Lamar Cooper Postcard Collection (PI/1992.0001, no. 30), courtesy of the Mississippi Department of Archives and History.

p. 138 First Baptist Church (IV), McComb (1923–24). From a postcard in the collection of the author.

p. 139 Temple Beth Israel (I), Meridian (circa 1875). From the Meridian City Directory, 1888, courtesy of the Historic Preservation Division, Mississippi Department of Archives and History.

p. 140 Church of the Mediator (Episcopal), Meridian (1876–78). Photograph by E. von Seutter (PI/1985.0032, no. 68), courtesy of the Mississippi Department of Archives and History.

p. 140 Church of the Mediator (engraving). From the Meridian City Directory, 1888, courtesy of the Historic Preservation Division, Mississippi Department of Archives and History.

p. 142 Central (First) Methodist Church, Meridian (1885). From a postcard, courtesy of the Historic Preservation Division, Mississippi Department of Archives and History.

p. 143 Central (First) Methodist Church, Meridian (engraving). From the Meridian City Directory, 1888, courtesy of the Historic Preservation Division, Mississippi Department of Archives and History.

p. 144 First Baptist Church, Meridian (1892–93). From a photograph in *Art Work of Mississippi* (1901), courtesy of the Mississippi Department of Archives and History.

p. 145 First Baptist Church, Meridian (1892–93). WPA photograph courtesy of the Historic Preservation Division, Mississippi Department of Archives and History.

p. 145 First Baptist Church, Meridian (1892–93). From a postcard in the collection of the author.

p. 146 Architectural perspective of Temple Beth Israel (II), Meridian (1906). From a postcard in the Postcard Negative Collection (PI/1985.0031, no. 694), courtesy of the Mississippi Department of Archives and History.

p. 146 Temple Beth Israel (II), Meridian. WPA photograph courtesy of the Historic Preservation Division, Mississippi Department of Archives and History.

p. 148 Pine Ridge Presbyterian Church, near Natchez (1828). Photograph courtesy of the Historic Preservation Division, Mississippi Department of Archives and History.

p. 149 Clear Creek Baptist Church, near Natchez (1828). Photograph (PI/CH/1982.0063, no. 2), courtesy of the Mississippi Department of Archives and History.

p. 150 First Baptist Church, New Albany (1898–99). From a postcard in the Postcard Negative Collection (PI/1985.0031, no. 729), courtesy of the Mississippi Department of Archives and History.

p. 151 Perspective No. 49. From Benjamin D. Price and Max Charles Price, *Church Plans* (1906).

p. 152 First Methodist Church, Newton (circa 1900–4?). WPA photograph (from PI/WPA/SF/Newton), courtesy of the Mississippi Department of Archives and History.

p. 153 First Baptist Church, Newton (1908). WPA photograph (in PI/WPA/SF/Newton), courtesy of the Mississippi Department of Archives and History.

p. 154 First Baptist Church, Oxford (1881–82). From a postcard in the Postcard Negative Collection (PI/1985.0031, no. 754), courtesy of the Mississippi Department of Archives and History.

p. 156 First Presbyterian Church, Pascagoula (1896). From a postcard in a private collection.

p. 158 Trinity Episcopal Church, Pass Christian (circa 1849). From a postcard in the Robert S. Conrich Collection (PI/1984.0012, no. 4), courtesy of the Mississippi Department of Archives and History.

p. 159 Trinity Episcopal Church, Pass Christian (exterior and interior). From a postcard in the Forrest Lamar Cooper Postcard Collection (PI/1992.0001, no. 1081), courtesy of the Mississippi Department of Archives and History.

p. 160 St. Paul's Catholic Church, Pass Christian (1879). From a postcard in the Forrest Lamar Cooper Postcard Collection (PI/1992.0001, no. 1080), courtesy of the Mississippi Department of Archives and History.

p. 162 Carolina Presbyterian Church, southwest of Philadelphia (1842). WPA photograph (PI/CO/N48, no. 48), courtesy of the Mississippi Department of Archives and History.

p. 163 First Baptist Church, Philadelphia (1926). WPA photograph (PI/CO/N48, no. 50), courtesy of the Mississippi Department of Archives and History.

p. 164 Zion Baptist Church, near Pontotoc. WPA photograph (from PI/WPA/SF/Pontotoc County [2]), courtesy of the Mississippi Department of Archives and History.

p. 166 Toxish Baptist Church, near Pontotoc (1905). WPA photograph of exterior (PI/CO/1982.0074, no. 3), courtesy of the Mississippi Department of Archives and History.

p. 167 Toxish Baptist Church, near Pontotoc. WPA photograph of interior (PI/CO/1982.0074, no. 2), courtesy of the Mississippi Department of Archives and History.

p. 168 "Old Magnolia Church," near Port Gibson (circa 1845–1850?). WPA photograph, courtesy of the Historic Preservation Division, Mississippi Department of Archives and History.

p. 169 First Baptist Church, Ripley (1916). WPA photograph (from PI/WPA/SF/Ripley), courtesy of the Mississippi Department of Archives and History.

p. 170 Presbyterian Church, Scooba (circa 1895–1900). WPA photograph (from PI/WPA/SF/Kemper County [1]), courtesy of the Mississippi Department of Archives and History.

p. 171 Perspective Nos. 183, 183A, and 183C. From Benjamin D. Price and Max Charles Price, *Church Plans* (1906).

p. 172 First Methodist Church, Senatobia (1880). From a postcard in the Forrest Lamar Cooper Postcard Collection (PI/1992.0001, no. 4190), courtesy of the Mississippi Department of Archives and History.

p. 173 First Methodist Church, Senatobia, about 1950. From a postcard in the collection of the author.

p. 174 First Methodist Church, Shelby (1912). From a postcard in the Forrest Lamar Cooper Postcard Collection (PI/1992.0001, no. 3093), courtesy of the Mississippi Department of Archives and History.

p. 174 Perspective No. 141B. From Benjamin D. Price and Max Charles Price, *Church Plans* (1906).

p. 176 First Presbyterian Church, Starkville (1855). From a postcard in the collection of the author. (There is a photograph of the same postcard in the Postcard Negative Collection (PI/1985.0031, no. 818) of the Mississippi Department of Archives and History.

p. 177 (Original) Crawford Street Methodist Church, Vicksburg (1846). Photograph in the Vicksburg Photographs Collection (PI/CI/V53.5, no. 270), courtesy of the Mississippi Department of Archives and History.

p. 178 (Original) Crawford Street Methodist Church, Vicksburg, in 1899. Photograph in the Warren County Glass Plates Collection (PI/2000.0004, no. 38), courtesy of the Mississippi Department of Archives and History.

p. 178 (Original) Crawford Street Methodist Church, Vicksburg, being demolished. Photograph in the Warren County Glass Plates Collection (PI/2000.0004, no. 61), courtesy of the Mississippi Department of Archives and History.

p. 179 St. Paul's Catholic Church, Vicksburg (circa 1850). From a postcard in the Forrest Lamar Cooper Postcard Collection (PI/1992.0001, no. 2849), courtesy of the Mississippi Department of Archives and History.

p. 180 St. Mary's Catholic Church , Natchez. From a postcard in the Forrest Lamar Cooper Postcard Collection (PI/1992.0001, no. 2042), courtesy of the Mississippi Department of Archives and History.

p. 180 St. Alphonsus Catholic Church, Baltimore, Maryland. From a postcard in the collection of the author.

p. 181 St. Paul's Catholic Church, Vicksburg, in the 1930s. WPA photograph in the Vicksburg Photographs Collection (PI/CI/V53.5, no. 116), courtesy of the Mississippi Department of Archives and History.

p. 182 First Presbyterian Church, Vicksburg (1855). From a postcard in the Forrest Lamar Cooper Postcard Collection (PI/1992.0001, no. 2830), courtesy of the Mississippi Department of Archives and History.

p. 184 First Baptist Church, Vicksburg (1878–79/1906–7). Photograph courtesy of the Old Court House Museum, Vicksburg.

p. 186 First Baptist Church, Vicksburg, in 1938. WPA photograph in the Vicksburg Photographs Collection (PI/CI/V53.5, no. 121), courtesy of the Mississippi Department of Archives and History.

p. 187 Bethel A.M.E. Church, Vicksburg (1879). Photograph courtesy of the Old Court House Museum, Vicksburg.

p. 188 Crawford Street Methodist Church, Vicksburg (1899). From a postcard in the collection of the author.

p. 189 Crawford Street Methodist Church. Photograph courtesy of the Old Court House Museum, Vicksburg.

p. 190 Crawford Street Methodist Church, with addition. From a postcard in the collection of the author.

p. 190 Presbyterian Church, Gainesville, Texas. From a postcard in the collection of the author.

p. 190 Grace Methodist Church, Dallas, Texas. From a postcard in the collection of the author.

p. 191 Crawford Street Methodist Church, after the fire of 1925. Photograph courtesy of the Old Court House Museum, Vicksburg.

p. 192 Church of the Nativity (Episcopal), Water Valley (circa 1895, 1918). WPA photograph (PI/SF/CH/1986.0033, no. 19), courtesy of the Mississippi Department of Archives and History.

p. 193 Perspective No. 42 and 42A. From Benjamin D. Price and Max Charles Price, *Church Plans* (1906).

p. 194 First Baptist Church, West Point (1888). From a postcard in the Forrest Lamar Cooper Postcard Collection (PI/1992.0001, no. 3748), courtesy of the Mississippi Department of Archives and History.

p. 195 First Baptist Church, West Point, in the 1930s. WPA photograph (Official Records Series 1631, no. 200), courtesy of the Mississippi Department of Archives and History.

p. 196 First Baptist Church, West Point, being demolished, 1985. Photograph courtesy of the Historic Preservation Division, Mississippi Department of Archives and History.

p. 197 Presbyterian Church, West Point (1898). WPA photograph (Official Records Series 1631, no. 212), courtesy of the Mississippi Department of Archives and History.

p. 199 First Presbyterian Church, Yazoo City (1887–88). From a photograph in *Art Work of Mississippi* (1901), courtesy of the Mississippi Department of Archives and History.

p. 200 First Baptist Church, Yazoo City (1904). From a postcard in the Forrest Lamar Cooper Postcard Collection (PI/1992.0001, no. 3222), courtesy of the Mississippi Department of Archives and History.

p. 201 St. Stephen's Methodist Church, Yazoo City (circa 1904). From a photograph in *Yazoo County Story* (Fort Worth, Tex.: University Supply & Equipment Co., 1958), in a private collection.

Index